AIR PLANE TALK ©

CAPTAIN CARLSON'S

AIR PLANE TALK ©

By

GLENN E. CARLSON

 Watosh Publishing, Las Vegas, Nevada

CAPTAIN CARLSON'S

AIR PLANE TALK ©

By GLENN E. CARLSON

THE COMPLETE BOOK OF
VFR AND IFR COMMUNICATIONS

WORKING THE ATC SYSTEM

●

Second Printing — March, 1984
Third Printing — March, 1985

Cover By — Douglas Nielson
Edited By — Linda C. Carlson

Graphics and Illustrations By — Herb Ferro
Las Vegas, Nevada

Library of Congress
Catalog Number - TX 1-077-924

ISBN 0-9611954-0-1

Printed and Bound in the
United States of America

WATOSH PUBLISHING
P.O. Box 11231
Las Vegas, Nevada 89111

To My Wife

TABLE OF CONTENTS

Author's Note 1
Introduction 2

CHAPTER I   An Introduction to the Airport ...   3
                   The Control Tower   3
                   The Runway   4
                   The Traffic Pattern   6

CHAPTER II   Basic Airport Communication ... 10
                   Your Call Sign 10
                   Where Are You? 12
                   What Do You Want? 14
                   The ATIS..................... 23

CHAPTER III   VFR Arrivals and Departures 30
                   Departing the Traffic Pattern 30
                   The Airport Traffic Area 32
                   Entering The Traffic Pattern 36

CHAPTER IV   Tower Separation Techniques ... 48
                   Operation Lights On............ 52
                   Split Frequencies............... 53

CHAPTER V   Uncontrolled Fields............. 56
                   Tower Closed 56
                   The Flight Service Station....... 60
                   Unicom and Multicom 63

CHAPTER VI   The Transponder.   66

CHAPTER VII   Terminal Control Areas   70

CHAPTER VIII   The Control Zone   82
                    Special VFR   84

CHAPTER IX   Radar   90
                    Stage Service   90
                    Traffic Advisories.   94

CHAPTER X   VFR Flight Plan   98

CHAPTER XI   Weather Briefings En Route   104

CHAPTER XII   Emergencies   106
                    The DF Steer   110
                    Skyjacking.   113

CHAPTER XIII   VFR Flight Following   114
                    Helping ATC.   116

CHAPTER XIV   One Way Communications   121
                    Pilot Controlled Lighting   121
                    No Radio.   122
                    Partial Communications Failure. . . .   123

CHAPTER XV   Instrument Flight Communications   125
                    IFR Airspace.   125
                    IFR Handoffs   130
                    The IFR Flight Plan and the Tower
                    En Route Clearance   132

CHAPTER XVI The ATC Clearance 133
       Essential Elements in a Clearance 134
       VFR Restrictions in IFR Flight ... 137
       Pre-flight Planning.............. 138

CHAPTER XVII IFR Departure Procedures....... 142

CHAPTER XVIII En Route Procedures 156
       Operation in Restricted Airspace 161
       Holding 162
       ATC Holding Instructions 166
       Lost Communications.......... 170
       Holding Pattern Airspace........ 171

CHAPTER XIX IFR Arrival Procedures.......... 173
       The Star...................... 173
       Flow Control 173
       Approach Control 174
       Cancellation of the IFR Flight Plan 177
       Approach Clearance........... 182
       Procedure Turns 188
       Radar Vectoring............... 191
       Timed Approaches From
       a Holding Fix 194
       Radar Approaches............. 194
       Radar Monitoring of
       Instrument Approaches 198

CHAPTER XIX   Simultaneous ILS Approaches . . 200

Parallel Approaches 201

The Side Step Maneuver 202

Missed Approach 202

Contact and Visual Approaches . . 203

Landing Priority 207

Pop Up Clearances 208

GLOSSARY 211

AUTHOR'S NOTE

This book is about talking on the aircraft radio. Progressing from your first flight lesson to advanced utilization of the Air Traffic Control system, this book is a step by step explanation of what to say, what will be told to you, and how you should respond.

To some readers, the contents will be their first introduction to "How it's done". To others, the information here will serve as a review. For those contemplating a career in aviation, be it as a pilot, or an air traffic controller, this book will introduce you to one of the most important aspects of these jobs — the skill of communication.

My hope is that you will become acquainted with the entire Air Traffic Control system and use it as legally intended, with confidence and understanding. My intent is to teach today's pilot the secrets of sounding and acting like a professional and competent airman.

 Captain G.E. Carlson

INTRODUCTION

Everyone who operates an aircraft transceiver, (transmitter and receiver), must have a radio operators permit. This permit is called a Restricted Radiotelephone Operator Permit, and is issued by the Federal Communications Commission. There are also more advanced licenses such as those that are issued to Ham radio operators or professional broadcasters. There are many reasons why we must be licensed, but for now just remember that it is the law! Your flight instructor will get the required forms for you and show you how to fill them out. You must have the license in your possession before you solo and until then you are talking on your instructor's license.

The F.A.A. tells us that the aircraft radio is a radiotelephone and should be used as a telephone to communicate our wishes. They mean that the correct phraseology is not mandatory and that it is acceptable to speak in layman's terms if you're lost for words. I tell my students that sounding professional on the radio will get you places more expeditiously than if you sound like a bumpkin. A perfect example is the fellow who was learning to fly back home on the farm and decided to take a cross country flight to the Los Angeles basin. He was so overwhelmed by the Stage III communications, and tied up the frequency so long, that when he was finally handed over to the tower, an unidentified and frustrated voice said, "welcome to the big city, Farmer." He wouldn't have been so easily picked out as a bungler and his cross country would have gone much smoother if he had only been more comfortable with his radio work. These are the types of problems I hope to help you conquer with this book.

CAPTAIN CARLSON'S AIRPLANE TALK
Chapter I
An Introduction To The Airport

The Control Tower

Most control towers are run by the F.A.A. although there are a few that are owned by private corporations. We will concern ourselves primarily with the more common F.A.A. tower.

The number of people who staff a control tower varies depending on how busy the facility is. The number of take-offs and landings, and IFR approaches made by general aviation, military, and commercial airliner type aircraft is recorded each day, week, month, and year. Every time an aircraft is cleared for take-off or cleared to land, the tower person who clears the aircraft punches a button on a counter. This count is very important because it dictates the necessity for buying fancy new equipment. It determines the need for length of operating hours that a tower is open, whether or not radar, extra lighting, or an ILS are needed. It also corresponds to the degree of difficulty of the job and the government service scale wages that will be paid.

There are two basic positions in every control tower, **Local Control** and **Ground Control.** The **Local Controller** handles all aircraft in the air or those that are awaiting take-off clearance. The **Ground Controller** handles all aircraft taxiing to or from the active runway or anywhere else on the field. Both the **Ground Controller** and the **Local Controller** are physically located in the glass house known as the control tower. They talk on different frequencies, because they have different responsibilities. Each controller takes turns at each position to add a little variety to their jobs. Initially you might feel that **Local Control** is more difficult than **Ground Control.** That is not always the case. In some of the nation's busiest airports like LAX, JFK, or ORD, the **Ground Control** is the most confusing. In contrast, satellite airports of major cities like SNA, the John Wayne Orange County airport, or SJC, San Jose Municipal airport, the **Local Control** is more difficult. Here, **Local Control** must keep light, slower moving aircraft and fast, heavy, jet aircraft separated and organized. It is when operating in high density airports that this book will prove most helpful. The tower is a welcome asset at hundreds of traffic saturated airports around the nation.

The one thing that has distinguished airports from any other piece of real estate is the runway, our next subject.

The Runway

All airports large or small have one thing in common — runways. Runways range from grass and dirt to super stressed concrete for heavy jets. Hard surfaced runways are numbered for ease of identification. For example, think of an imaginary airport with two runways (two giant slabs of concrete). See diagram A. We will call them 36L

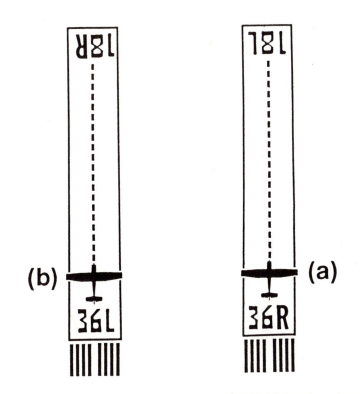

Diagram "A"

(pronounced three six left) and 36R (pronounced three six right). They get their names because of the magnetic heading they best represent, within five degrees. If an airplane sits on 36R like aircraft A, it's heading is approximately 360 degrees or North. In reality, the compass in aircraft A might read 356 degrees to 004 degrees, but technically it's heading closely approximates magnetic North. Why the left and right designation? Well aircraft B is on the parallel runway to the left. A few airports in the country have three runways, all parallel. In this case, the F.A.A. may designate 36C (center). Another option is to designate one of the outside parallel runways the next possible runway number (35 or 01).

In diagram A, the other end of the runways are labeled 18R (pronounced one eight right), and 18L (one eight left) because their magnetic heading approximates 180 degrees (South).

Control towers direct arriving and departing traffic to and from the runways by utilizing the concept of the traffic pattern.

The Traffic Pattern

The traffic pattern is an imaginary rectangle. Each **leg** of the rectangle has a name. Refer to diagram B. Common sense was applied in their naming. One concept that has been around since the Wright Brothers is that the pilot should always take-off and land flying into the wind, **headwind** produces the slowest ground speed and con-

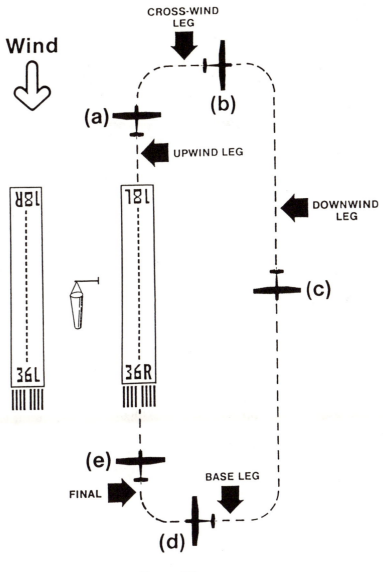

Wind

CROSS-WIND LEG

(a)

(b)

UPWIND LEG

DOWNWIND LEG

18R

18L

36L

36R

(c)

(e)

BASE LEG

FINAL

(d)

Diagram "B"

Page 7

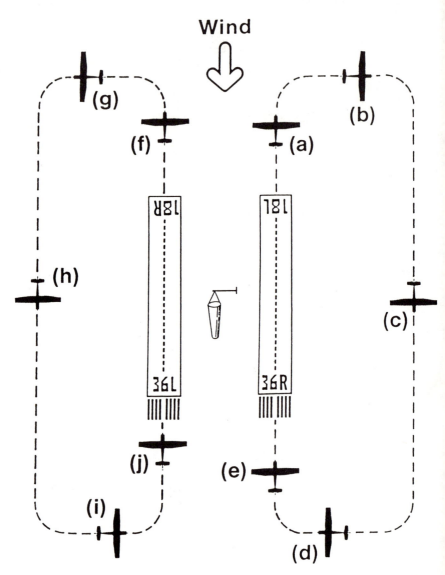

Diagram "C"

sequently the shortest landing and take-off roll. Aircraft A is on the **upwind** leg. Aircraft B is on the **crosswind** leg which gets it's name because his flight path is perpendicular or crosswind to the rectangle. Aircraft C is flying on the **downwind** leg because the wind is behind him. He's flying with the wind. Aircraft D is now crosswind by definition, but it would be confusing to have two crosswind legs in the same traffic pattern, consequently the name assigned to this leg is the **base** leg. Aircraft E is on his final leg before landing so this leg is called **final,** even though the aircraft is upwind. As we look at the first five aircraft (abcde) in diagram C flying the traffic pattern, it is plain to see that all five aircraft must turn right in order to fly this pattern. They are flying **right traffic.** Conversely, aircraft f, g, h, i, and j are flying **left traffic** because they are making left turns. It is essential that you be able to picture in your mind the position of each aircraft and be able to know the correct name for each leg.

The next chapter deals with basic airport communications. The section deals primarily with the radio work associated with aircraft taxiing about the airport. It is the foundation for all phases of radio communication.

Chapter II

Basic Airport Communication

Your Call Sign

Your flight instructor will tell you that the essentials of talking on the radio include three basic pieces of information: who you are, where you are, and what you want.

Who you are is explained by using your aircraft "N" number. All aircraft registered in the United States have a number assigned to them that begins with the letter "N". If your aircraft is registered in Canada, your registration number would begin with the letters "CA", in Mexico "XA". Other countries use two letters to designate national registry. If you are flying a U.S. registered aircraft within the United States, the "N" preceeding your number is presumed unless you specify otherwise. When used, the letter "N" is communicated as "November". The International Civil Aviation Organization, which was formed by the nations of the free world, adopted English as the international language for aviation communications. The ICAO (pronounced I KAY O) established a phonetic alphabet for radio transmissions. The phonetic alphabet uses words to replace letters. Each word was chosen carefully to avoid the chance of being mistaken for another word. The ICAO also adopted standard methods of reciting numbers. Most single numbers are pronounced the same except for the number 9, which is spoken as "niner" so as not to be confused with the German word "nein", which means "no". The number five is pronounced "fife". Numbers of two or more digits are spoken as a series of single digits, except for round numbers such as hundreds and thousands. Examples of the phonetic alphabet and number pronounciations are listed below.

A	Alpha	N	November
B	Bravo	O	Oscar
C	Charlie	P	Papa
D	Delta	Q	Quebec
E	Echo	R	Romeo
F	Foxtrot	S	Sierra
G	Golf	T	Tango
H	Hotel	U	Uniform
I	India	V	Victor
J	Juliett	W	Whiskey
K	Kilo	X	Xray
L	Lima	Y	Yankee
M	Mike	Z	Zulu

25	two fife	0600	zero six hundred
876	eight seven six	2,800	two thousand eight hundred
900	niner hundred	14,000	one four thousand
		19,521	one niner thousand fife two one

Your aircraft type along with the registration number becomes your **call sign.** An example of an aircraft **call sign** might be, Cessna 1740G and would be spoken on the radio as "Cessna one seven four zero Golf".

Stating the type of aircraft by model or by the manufacturers name preceding your registration number further aids ATC in indentifying you. You could be one of perhaps thousands of aircraft operating at a particular airport on any given day. When pilots state the model specifically by saying, "Skyhawk" rather than Cessna, they are indicating that they are flying a Cessna 172. If "Skylane" is used they are in a Cessna 182. Piper Cherokee pilots say "Cherokee", but some say "Arrow" because "Arrow" is the specific model of Cherokee. Pilots of Cessna models 310, 402, 421, etc., often say "Twin Cessna..." because they are similar in appearance and have two engines. The more time you spend around airports, the easier it will be to recognize all these types of aircraft by name. There aren't really any hard and fast rules here, but you should learn to recognize the terminology and realize that any little bit of identification is helpful. When you have told the tower what type of aircraft you are in and your registration number, the next step is to say where you are.

Where Are You?

Often there are so many aircraft at an airport that if you don't tell the controller where you are it could take considerable time to find you. You must be very specific when describing your location. If you are learning to fly at Ace Flying School, you might just tell the controller that you are at "Ace". See diagram D. *At some airports the controllers are familiar with most of the local airplanes and their "N" numbers, so they might know where you are even if you get flustered and forget.*

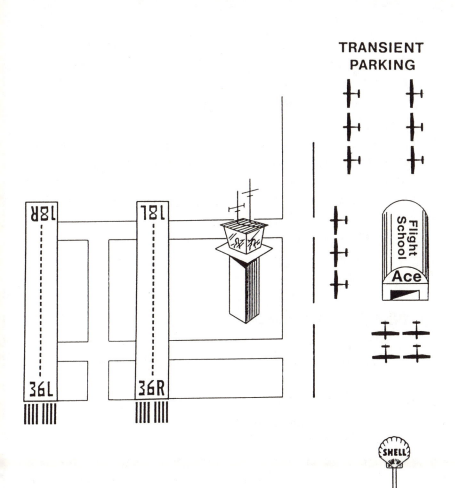

TRANSIENT PARKING

Flight School Ace

GAS

Diagram "D"

If you are refueling for the next segment of your trip and there are several gas pits on the field, you must be specific and tell the controller your position is the "Shell" pit (meaning you are in the Shell gas area). If you are on a cross country flight and are just passing through, you might advise the controller that you are parked in the transient parking area. Some airports may have many transient parking areas. *If you are on the ball, the first thing you might do after you have started the engine, is to set your gyro compass to orient yourself accurately on the field.* When you call Ground Control, you could say, "I'm in transient parking, west of the tower, or north of Ace Flying School...".

What Do You Want?

After you have told the controller who you are and where you are, he will be interested in <u>what you want to do</u>, or <u>what you want to know</u>, or why you are calling! First, in order to talk to the appropriate controller, you must know the correct channel or **frequency.** Your instructor will give you the Ground Control frequency for your airport and later he will teach that any other unknown **frequencies** can be looked up in the Airman's Information Manual Airport/Facility Directory. Now let's try an example using diagram D.

You: "Buchanan Ground Control, Cessna one two three four Bravo, transient parking, taxi to the Shell pit."

Ground Control: "Cessna three four Bravo, taxi to the Shell pit."

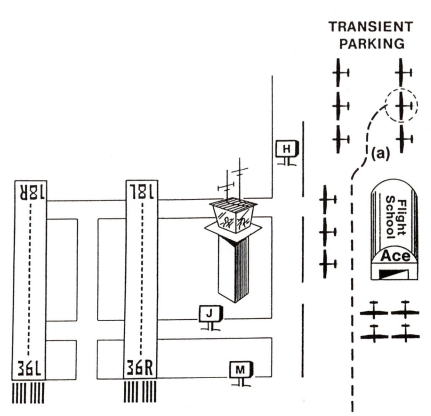

Diagram "E"

The pilot should always use the name of the airport that he is talking to. *In this case, I used the name Buchanan because Buchanan Field is an airport dear to my heart.* To break this dialogue into fundamentals, you said, "Buchanan Ground Control..." because that is who you wish to speak to. "Cessna one two three four Bravo" is who you are. On your initial call up, you use your full five call letters. In subsequent transmissions you may shorten your name to "Cessna three four Bravo". "Transient parking, taxi to the Shell pit..." means you want to go to the fuel pit and gas up. Realistically, the controller doesn't care what you are going to do once you get there, he is only concerned with the fact that you want permission to travel from the transient parking area to the Shell pit. Ground Control came back and said, "Cessna three four Bravo, taxi to the Shell pit", indicating that you may taxi to the gas pit by any route you wish. Often, however his final remarks may include directions such as, "...taxi to the Shell pit via the ramp..." (via is Latin which means "by the way of"). The **ramp** is the area where the planes are parked. The controller is always concerned with traffic so he may have a good reason for wanting you to use the ramp, as in path A in diagram E.

Path A in diagram F would be directions from the controller, "...taxi to the Shell pit via the outer...". He means, use the outer taxi way, not the ramp. You must listen carefully and have the directions clear in your mind.

One aspect of good radio work is not to shout at the controller.

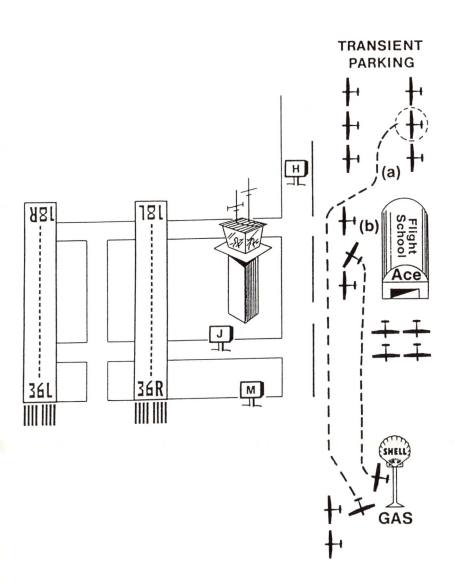

Diagram "F"

Even though you may have a hard time hearing yourself over the engine noise, it is best to talk in a calm, clear voice. If you shout, it often sounds panicky. Try to imagine how it would be to listen to shouting all day. Controllers can tell a lot by your voice so try not to sound nervous and excited, your inexperience will show. Always try to be courteous and listen so that you do not try to talk at the same time as another pilot. If two pilots transmit at the same time, the controller will not be able to understand either of you. He will hear only a loud squeal and will respond by saying, "Two aircraft attempting transmission at the same time, one at a time please." Wait until the controller is finished with the first pilot before you attempt to speak.

You may encounter a change in instructions because of another aircraft calling up, so be prepared. Here is an example.

Cessna 65A:	"Ground, Cessna six five Alpha, Shell pit, taxi to Ace."
Ground Control:	"Cessna six five Alpha taxi via the ramp. Break. Cessna three four Bravo, turn right, taxi to the Shell pit via the outer."
Cessna 65A:	"Six five Alpha."
You:	"Three four Bravo."

If we analyze this fast paced transmission, referring again to diagram F, we can see that Ground Control had to make some quick changes. First of all, in diagram E, Ground Control was perfectly happy to let you taxi to the gas pit via the ramp taxiway. Then, when Cessna 65A called from the fuel pit and wanted to taxi to the Ace Flight School, the controller could quickly see that if each aircraft continued in the opposite direction toward each other, somewhere in front of Ace Flight School they would meet head on. *Few aircraft have the ability to back up. Each pilot would have to shut down their engines and with a tow bar push their aircraft out of each other's way.* The controller quickly decided to let Cessna 65A taxi to his parking spot via the ramp. At the same time he decided this, he saw you rapidly approaching the entrance to the ramp in front of Ace. If he didn't get you to turn right, quickly, you wouldn't be able to avoid the head on confrontation. *If you were real sharp you would have heard all of this coming and started to slow down in anticipation of altered instructions.* Anticipating the possible confrontation, ATC told Cessna 65A to taxi and then said, "Break", (which means to wait a minute to acknowledge my last transmission, I have to give a quick message to another aircraft). The controller asked you to turn right and taxi via the outer. Both aircraft should then acknowledge Ground Control by answering in the order of whom was spoken to first. Since Cessna 65A was spoken to first, he acknowledges first, then you. It will take time to get the hang of it so be patient with yourself and "Listen up". O.K., so much for taxiing around the airport, let's go somewhere.

Suppose that you are learning to fly at the Ace Flight School. You are in a Cessna 182 and have started your engine.

You: "Ground, Cessna one two three four Bravo, Ace ramp, taxi for take-off."

It is permissable to just say "Ground" or "Tower", but be sure you are on the correct frequency. Imagine the confusion that would follow if you received taxi or landing instructions from a different tower located ten miles away! Ground Control might come back and say, "Cessna three four Bravo, standby." If he says "Standby", then he is probably busy and must direct all of his attention to a particular problem with taxiing aircraft. He may be so busy that he didn't have time to write down your aircraft number on his scratch pad so he might say, "Aircraft calling for taxi, say again your call sign." You don't have to repeat your whole longwinded transmission. All you have to say is, "Cessna one two three four Bravo." Ground Control is now able to continue with the numbers, "Cessna three four Bravo taxi to runway three six right, wind zero two zero at ten, altimeter three zero zero one, taxi via the outer." *This all comes pretty fast. It is best for you to have a scratch pad ready so you can write down what he says. The controller will always give you this information in the same order.* First, you were given the runway assignment, 36R. then the wind, 020 at 10, meaning that the wind is coming from 020 degrees, which in this case is a 20 degree crosswind at ten knots. The wind direction, called surface wind, is given in magnetic direction to correspond to the runway direction. *It is helpful to use your gyro compass to help find the runway and assess the crosswind component.*

As you sit in front of Ace, in diagram G, you set your directional gyro and see that if you take off on runway 36 you will be heading North, so, you must taxi South to get to the end of the runway. The altimeter setting is then placed in the window of your altimeter. Your altimeter may not read the exact field elevation as published on your sectional chart because airports, especially the larger ones, have varied heights throughout the airport's bound- ries. So long as your indication is close to published

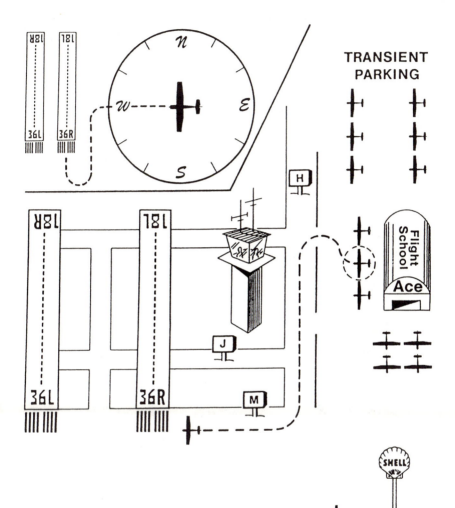

Diagram "G"

heights, one need not be concerned. The F.A.A. has set up accuracy standards for altimeters used for IFR flight only.

The controller may give you very specific directions to runway 36R. He may say, "Taxi to three six right via Hotel and Mike." In this case, you taxi as in diagram G. Taxiways are often given names in the form of letters in the alphabet and then put on little signs that are often hard to see. If you are a new pilot, or new to an airport and don't think you can find the correct taxiway say, "I'm unfamiliar, request **progressive taxi instructions.**" You have just told the controller that you don't know your way around the airport and would like to be led by the hand out to the runway. There is no disgrace in asking for this kind of help. Professional pilots do it unabashedly, and often. "Request progressive taxi", is just a more professional way of saying, "I'm confused and could use some help." "I'm unfamiliar", is the brief standard way of saying, "I don't know my way around this airport." Air traffic controllers are there to help and they do a pretty good job if they know the situation.

Let's back up a bit and put ourselves back at the Ace Flight School ramp. We are just about to call Ground Control, when another aircraft calls up and says, "Buchanan Ground, Cherokee six niner five five Charlie, transient parking, taxi for take-off."

ATC: "Cherokee five five Charlie, taxi to runway three six right, wind zero two zero at ten, altimeter three zero zero one."

Cherokee 6955C: "Five five Charlie."

Now if you are sharp, you will have copied the details given the other pilot. When you call up you say, "Buchanan Ground, Cessna one two three four Bravo, Ace ramp, taxi for take-off with the numbers." This phrase tells the controller that you heard what was told to the Cherokee and don't need a repeat. The controller will say, "Cessna three four Bravo, taxi to runway three six right." You have saved his breath and he will appreciate the fact that he does not have to keep repeating the runway, wind and altimeter.

The ATIS

There are airports that are so busy that they have a tape recorder like transmitter installed called an ATIS (Automatic Terminal Information Service). Check your sectional chart and the ATIS frequency will be listed along with the other information. You may listen to the recording as many times as you wish until you get all of the information. *Think. If the engine is not running, the battery is not being charged. If you turn on the master switch and continue to listen over and over again to the ATIS, you may run down the battery. If you have the engine running, the more you listen, the more it will cost you on the old Hobbs meter. Students seem to respond to a dollar and cents approach and soon learn to copy the ATIS with amazing speed.*

The ATIS information is usually updated every hour and is assigned a letter of the alphabet starting with "Alpha" in the morning and continuing to "Zulu" in the evening. It may remain the same for several hours if there is no significant change in the airport weather. Additional information is given in the ATIS such as cloud cover, visability, or if a taxiway or runway is closed due to construction. The ATIS is helpful to the student by allowing a little more time to think.

When calling Ground Control say, "Ground, Cessna one two three four Bravo, Ace ramp, taxi for take-off with information Yankee." Ground Control will respond, "Cessna three four Bravo, taxi to runway three six left, hold short of the right at Mike." (As in diagram G.) In this case you have saved words using the ATIS code for the hour, "Yankee", and have saved time on the airwaves. You have been told to taxi to runway 36L. To quote the FAR's, "A clearance to taxi to a runway is a clearance to taxi across all runways to your assigned runway except you may not cross any active runways." Therefore you were told to taxi to runway 36L, but to **hold short** of 36R at taxiway Mike. There will be a double yellow hold line close to 36R and you may not cross it on your way to 36L until given clearance to do so. When you get close to 36R and the controller has not given you crossing permission yet, you can say, "Cessna three four Bravo, ready to cross the right." He will either say, "Cessna three four Bravo cross runway 36R, taxi to 36L." Or, "Cessna three four Bravo, hold short, traffic on short final." This means that there is an aircraft about to land on 36R and you must hold for him. This is shown in diagram H. After the aircraft lands, the controller will say, "Cessna three four Bravo cross the right, hold short of the left, contact tower after crossing." So you put the power to your flying machine, cross the right runway, and change to the tower frequency remem-

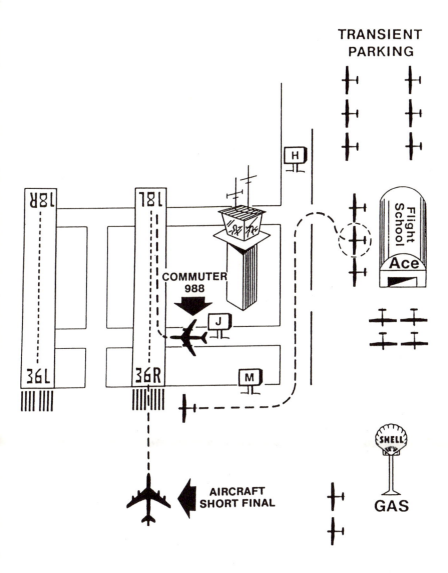

Diagram "H"

bering to hold short of the left runway. Now as we are holding short, have done our run-up, and are on the tower frequency, we may hear another type of transmission. Local Control calls a small commuter airline.

ATC: "Commuter nine eighty eight, will you require a run-up?"

Commuter 998: "Negative."

ATC: "Can you accept an intersection departure from Juliet? You will have 5,300 feet of runway remaining.

Commuter 998: "Affirm."

ATC: "Roger, cleared for immediate take-off, runway three six right, heavy jet traffic on a four mile final for the right."

Commuter 988: "Cleared for take-off, Commuter nine eighty eight."

What was that all about? Examine diagram H. First, the controller wanted to know if the commuter pilot needed a run-up. The pilot said, "Negative" (No). Actually, this pilot doesn't mean he's not going to do a run-up, because he must, but he means that he's already done it. To save time, sometimes a commuter pilot will do his run-up while taxiing out, so he doesn't have to wait in the run-up area. The next question asked by the controller was whether the pilot would like to make an intersection departure from taxiway Juliet. He would have to enter the runway from taxiway Juliet, taxi onto the runway and take-off. (As pictured in diagram H.) Along with his question, the controller let the pilot know how many feet of runway remained should the pilot elect to make the intersection departure. If the pilot feels that 5,300 feet of runway is adequate and safe for his type of aircraft, then he might accept the departure. In this case, the pilot said, "Affirm," (yes), indicating he would accept the intersection departure. Then the controller cleared the commuter for immediate take-off, his reason was that a jet had already been cleared to land. The jet was on a four mile final approach and he doesn't want them to get too close. So, the commuter pilot expeditiously takes the runway and takes off. *A couple of words of advice, first, don't do your run-ups while taxiing. When you are more experienced you will understand why I don't recommend this. Second, be careful about making intersection take-offs. If you are at a big airport and there is a 12,000 foot runway, that is certainly different than at an airport with a 6,000 foot runway.* If you don't want to make an intersection departure, don't. You just merely tell the controller, "We will need full length today." The controller can't make you do an intersection departure, so if you are not sure, don't do it! Just remember, the runway behind you is useless!

If Commuter 988 did not elect to accept the intersection departure, he would have to wait for "Back taxi" clearance to utilize the full length of the runway. "Back taxi" means to enter the runway from an intersection and taxi on the runway to the threshold. Back taxi clearances are usually accompanied by instructions to hold in position or to take-off. In this case, Commuter 988 would have to wait for the jet on short final to land before back taxi clearance would be issued. *"Back taxi" should not be confused with "taxi back". "Taxi back" means after executing a full stop landing, you would exit the runway and taxi back to the departure runway for another take-off.*

Let's get back to you in the run-up area, ready for take-off from 36L. You call the tower and say, "Buchanan tower, Cessna three four Bravo ready for take-off on the left." You have told him who you are, where you are, and what you want. It is very important that the controller know which runway you're at because, there may be many aircraft at both runways awaiting take-off clearance. Save time and further radio transmissions by saying, "the left" or "the right", or if there are multiple runways in use, 36 left or 36 right. Now the controller says, "Cessna three four Bravo cleared for take-off." You acknowledge by saying, "Three four Bravo." You are saying the same thing as "Roger", (I hear you and will comply). To say, "Three four Bravo, roger," is redundant. If you are not sure that the take-off clearance was for you, but you think it was, you can say, "Three four Bravo is cleared for take-off." If he doesn't answer with a "negative", then it was for you. If there is still some question in your mind say, "Verify Cessna three four Bravo was cleared for take-off." His answer, "Affirmative, Cessna three four Bravo cleared for take-off."

The next chapter deals with departures and arrivals to the traffic pattern and also incorporates discussion of the airport traffic area.

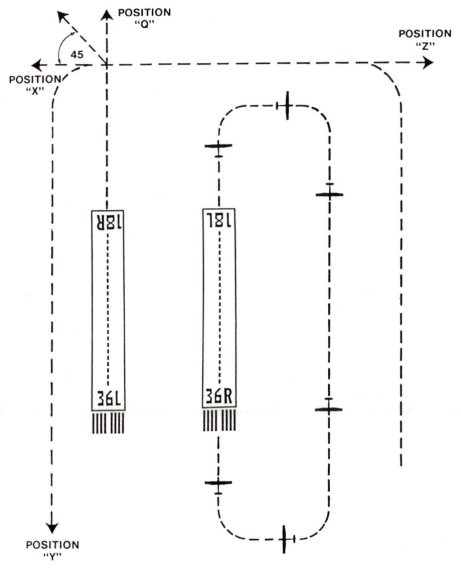

POSITION "Q"

POSITION "Z"

45

POSITION "X"

POSITION "Y"

18R

18L

36L

36R

Diagram "I"

Page 29

Chapter III
VFR ARRIVALS AND DEPARTURES

Departing the Traffic Pattern

When you take-off, the tower is assuming that your departure path will be to climb straight out until about 400 feet above ground level and then make a 45 degree turn and continue in that direction for five miles. The reason that you continue for five miles will be discussed later. Let's say you don't want to go that way after take-off but towards position X in diagram I. Then you would say, "...ready for take-off on the left, **request left cross wind departure.**" Air Traffic Control would say, "Left cross wind departure approved, cleared for take-off." So, you climb straight out until you reach a safe altitude, then make a left 90 degree turn, and continue for five miles. If instead, you want to head south towards position Y, then you would ask for a "**...left downwind departure.**" A departure towards position Q is called a **straight out departure**. If you want to go towards position Z you would request a **...Right crosswind departure.**" In this case the controller might say, "...continue straight out until advised, cleared for take-off." This means that he will tell you when it is O.K. to make your right 90 degree turn. He will wait until you are clear of all aircraft and then say, "Cessna three four Bravo, right turn approved." Regardless of what runway you are assigned, you can depart in a variety of ways because the tower will help you stay organized and separated from the other aircraft. Remember, it is still your responsibility to maintain Visual Flight Rules, (see and avoid), at all times. If you want to make a right 45 degree departure from the left runway, request a **right turn out**, as depicted in diagram J.

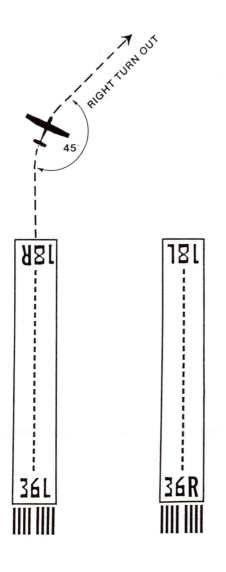

Diagram "J"

There are a few towers that use phrases like, "South departure approved," meaning, in the case of our imaginary airport, a left downwind departure is approved. "East departure approved," meaning right crosswind departure approved. This phraseology is not too common, but be listening for it. Helicopters use these terms frequently.

If you are in the "touch and go" phase of your flight training, and don't plan to leave the traffic pattern, then say, "...ready for take-off on the left, **request closed traffic**." You could also say, "...ready for take-off on the left, **remain in the pattern**." "**Closed traffic**" is more commonly used. Perhaps ATC wants to use 36R for touch and go traffic, then the tower might say, "Right closed traffic approved for 36R, cleared for take-off 36L." After take-off he wants you to fly your traffic pattern on 36R, so after take-off you turn right and fly a "right racetrack", as if you had taken off on 36R.

The Airport Traffic Area

It is essential that you know the difference between an airport traffic area and a control zone. Many pilots have difficulty understanding the difference and you need this knowledge to communicate effectively. The airport traffic area is an invisible cylinder around an airport that has an operating control tower. See diagram K. If an airport's control tower is open from 7 a.m. until 10 p.m. and you come in to land at 11 p.m., is there an airport traffic area? No! Why? Because the tower closed an hour previously, and even though there is a tower on the airport property, nobody's home in the little glass house. The airport traffic area is only in effect when the tower is open for business. Now, how big is this invisible cylinder? It has a five statute mile radius extending from the center of the airport. It

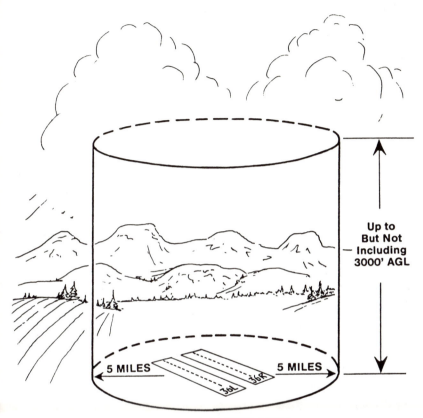

5 MILES ◄────────────────────────────► **5 MILES**

Up to
But Not
Including
3000' AGL

AIRPORT TRAFFIC AREA

Diagram "K"

starts at the surface and goes up to, but not including 3000 feet above ground level. O.K., now if we are flying over an airport and the tower is in operation, and the field elevation is 100 feet mean sea level, and your altimeter says you're at 3500 feet MSL, are you in the airport traffic area? The answer is No!! If your altimeter says 3099 feet or less you are in the airport traffic area. Federal Aviation Regulations tell us that you cannot operate within an airport traffic area without permission from the tower. Why? Because they have to have an area in which to work, to guarantee that everyone in that defined area is in radio communication with ATC. There is an exception to this rule, but we will cover this later.

Previously I mentioned that you are expected to continue your flight path after take-off until you are five miles from the airport. This is because the tower will warn other aircraft of your approximate position as well as warn you of the position of other aircraft.

Cessna 21216:	"Buchanan tower, Cessna two one two one six, seven miles north for landing with information Lima."
Tower:	"Cessna three four Bravo, traffic is a Cessna that just called seven north for 36L, break, Cessna two one six, traffic is a Cessna 182 four miles straight out from 36L."
You:	"Three four Bravo looking."
Cessna 21216:	"Two one six looking."
Tower:	"Cessna two one six report left downwind runway 36L."
Cessna 21216:	"Two one six request 36R."
Tower:	"I'll advise on left downwind."

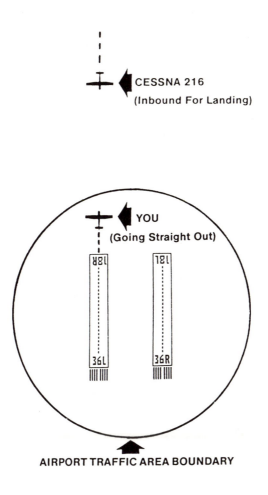

CESSNA 216
(Inbound For Landing)

YOU
(Going Straight Out)

18R 18L

36L 36R

AIRPORT TRAFFIC AREA BOUNDARY

Diagram "L"

The communications just mentioned, referring to diagram L, show why you must not deviate from your course before leaving the airport traffic area. The tower must be able to give airport advisories.

Entering the Traffic Pattern

Now let's talk about entering the airport traffic area for landing. First of all, let me reiterate that you may not enter the airport traffic area without a tower clearance to do so. Suppose you call the tower five miles out and it takes only thirty seconds for the tower to give you clearance. At the time your ground speed is 120 MPH. If you continue towards the airport while awaiting entry instructions, then you are technically already one mile <u>inside</u> the airport traffic area. If the tower is busy, it might be a good idea to call the tower between six and ten miles out so if ATC can't get back to you right away, you won't have to circle outside the five mile radius awaiting tower instructions. You should use one of the eight points of the compass when reporting your position. these eight points are: North, Northeast, East, Southeast, South, Southwest, West, and Northwest. See diagram M.

As you approach your destination airport, you should listen to the ATIS to determine the active runways in use. For our example, 36L and 36R are in use.

You:	"Buchanan tower, Cessna one two three four Bravo six east for landing with information Yankee."
Tower:	"Cessna three four Bravo report right downwind runway 36R."
You:	"Three four Bravo."

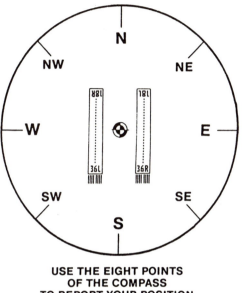

**USE THE EIGHT POINTS
OF THE COMPASS
TO REPORT YOUR POSITION
TO THE TOWER**

Diagram "M"

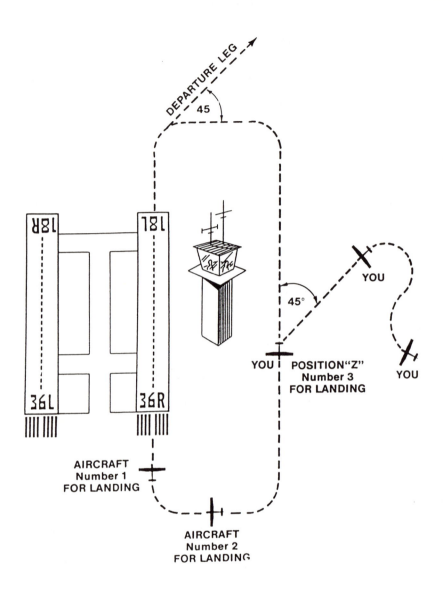

These instructions mean that you are expected to maneuver your flying machine so as to enter the downwind for the depicted 45 degree entry. See diagram N. Then you were told to report turning downwind. When reaching position Z in diagram N, you would say, "Cessna three four Bravo right downwind." If the tower is right off your right wing tip you can say, "Cessna three four Bravo right downwind **abeam**." **Abeam** is another way of saying that you are at a right angle to the tower. In this diagram the tower would then say, "Cessna three four Bravo, number three following the Cherokee on right base." The aircraft on final is number one to land, the Cherokee on right base is number two, and you are number three.

As we examine diagram O, let's try another situation.

You: "Buchanan tower, Cessna one two three four Bravo, six southeast for landing with Whiskey."

Tower: "Cessna three four Bravo report right base for 36R."

You: "Three four Bravo."

So you fly the maneuver as depicted and when you are at position Q you say, "Cessna three four Bravo, **wide right base.**"

Tower: "Cessna three four Bravo, in sight, number three following the Cherokee on close in right base."

You: "Three four Bravo."

Here we not only reported right base, but a wide right base. Why? Because here, we were wide, meaning farther away from the runway than aircraft Z. Aircraft Z is considered on a **close in** right base. Using terms such as, **wide** or **long** are relative judgement calls by the pilot or

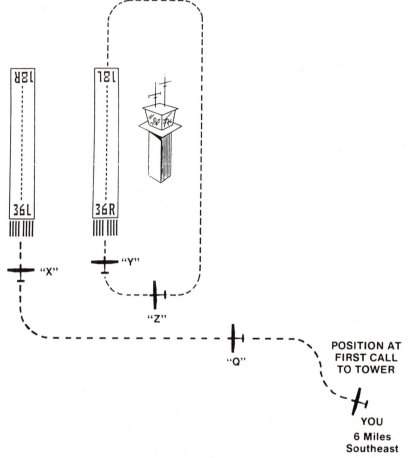

"X"

"Y"

"Z"

"Q"

POSITION AT
FIRST CALL
TO TOWER

YOU
6 Miles
Southeast

Diagram "O"

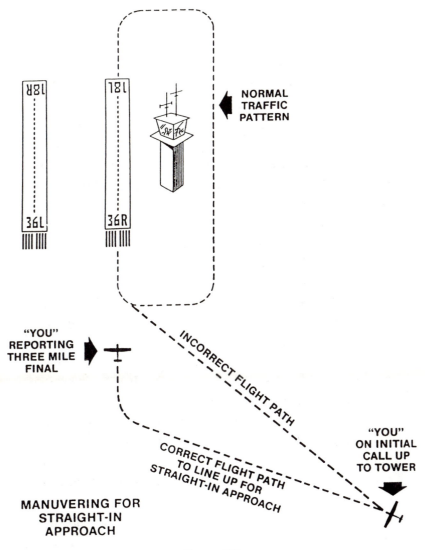

NORMAL
TRAFFIC
PATTERN

"YOU"
REPORTING
THREE MILE
FINAL

INCORRECT FLIGHT PATH

"YOU"
ON INITIAL
CALL UP
TO TOWER

CORRECT FLIGHT PATH
TO LINE UP FOR
STRAIGHT-IN APPROACH

MANUVERING FOR
STRAIGHT-IN
APPROACH

Diagram "P"

Page 41

the controller and helps both parties be more specific. If, after your original sequencing, the controller thinks you are too close to aircraft Z, he might say, "Cessna three four Bravo change to three six left, number two, follow the aircraft on short final for three six left." (The aircraft on short final is aircraft X on diagram O.) You respond. "Three four Bravo."

Now let's back up a bit and use the same situation. You have been told to make a right base entry to 36R but because of your position, you would rather go **straight in.** So you say, "Cessna three four Bravo, request straight in approach," or "Cessna three four Bravo, we'd like a straight in today." The tower responds, "Straight in approach approved, report three mile final." You should fly as shown in diagram P. You fly straight across until intersecting the center line of 36R before proceeding inbound. ATC requested the three mile final report to give himself enough time to organize the traffic flow. He may only want a two mile final report if traffic is light or you are a slow moving aircraft. One word of caution, don't 'cut the corner' to the three mile final point. The controller is expecting to first see your aircraft lined up straight in and not on a modified base leg entry. He may have conflicting traffic making a right base entry to 36R and he wouldn't be expecting you in the place you'd be in if you cut the corner.

Having a tower does not guarantee clearance for any kind of entry to the traffic pattern. For example, when you call up for landing ATC might say, "...report right downwind 36R."

You:	"...request right base or straight in."
Tower:	"...unable due to traffic." (Possible translation: I'm too busy to keep track of everyone so I want entry to the traffic pattern to be kept simple and easy.)

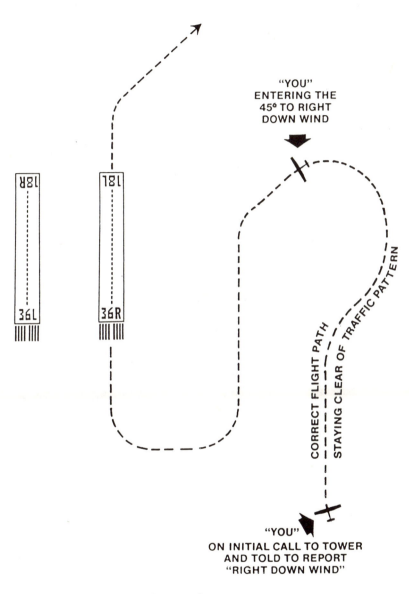

"YOU"
ENTERING THE
45° TO RIGHT
DOWN WIND

18R

18L

36L

36R

CORRECT FLIGHT PATH

STAYING CLEAR OF TRAFFIC PATTERN

"YOU"
ON INITIAL CALL TO TOWER
AND TOLD TO REPORT
"RIGHT DOWN WIND"

Diagram "Q"

Page 43

So you fly as depicted in diagram Q, making sure you don't get too close to the downwind leg, any downwind leg, including the wide downwind leg of jet aircraft. You don't have to skirt the five mile radius until in a position to enter as instructed, but, you do have to steer clear of all traffic in the pattern as you position yourself for the forty-five degree entry.

Remember, you may see people fly aircraft in all kinds of crazy ways, and you may never hear the tower scold a sloppy entry, but that doesn't mean it wasn't wrong. Set an example, do your entry correctly. Don't get caught under the FAR's "careless and reckless operation of aircraft" clause! Knowing what to say and what to expect to hear is half the battle in good radio work. Knowing where other aircraft are and where to expect them to be is half the battle in good, safe flying.

TPA stands for traffic pattern altitude, and for light aircraft it is usually eight hundred feet above ground level. I say usually, because some TPA's must be five hundred feet above ground level because they are under the flight path of a large major airport. There are no federal rules to govern traffic pattern altitudes. Customarily, it is usually fifteen hundred feet above ground level for jets, but don't count on that either. Years ago when jet fuel was cheap, jet aircraft would fly 1500 feet AGL traffic patterns all day long. Currently, most jet transports fly idle power descents from 35,000 feet all the way to about 1000 feet on final approach for fuel conservation. Jets will fly "chop and drop" or "slam dunk" traffic patterns so be on the look out and listen up.

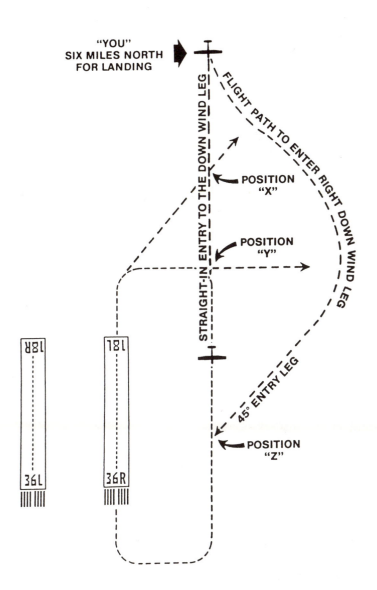

"YOU"
SIX MILES NORTH
FOR LANDING

FLIGHT PATH TO ENTER RIGHT DOWN WIND LEG

STRAIGHT-IN ENTRY TO THE DOWN WIND LEG

POSITION "X"

POSITION "Y"

45° ENTRY LEG

POSITION "Z"

18R

18L

36L

36R

Diagram "R"

Another situation to cover would be if you are six miles north for landing and are told to "...enter right downwind." See diagram R. As you can see, this maneuver will take some time to fly to the 45 degree entry leg. You also notice that the tower is not busy (because you have been monitoring the frequency for the last fifteen minutes), so when you are told to enter right downwind you say, "...request a straight in entry to the downwind leg." If he has no traffic he'll probably approve it. If the Local Controller were busy, he'd have to turn your request down because there are too many separation problems involved with this entry. You might have to avoid an aircraft departing at position X, crosswind traffic at position Y and 45 degree traffic at position Z. In short, that is why the 45 degree entry was invented.

Our next chapter deals with aircraft separation techniques used by the tower. In addition, we will touch upon the concepts of Operation Lights On and split frequencies.

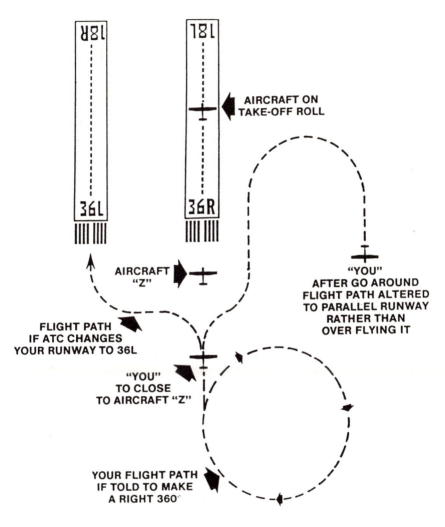

AIRCRAFT ON TAKE-OFF ROLL

AIRCRAFT "Z"

"YOU" AFTER GO AROUND FLIGHT PATH ALTERED TO PARALLEL RUNWAY RATHER THAN OVER FLYING IT

FLIGHT PATH IF ATC CHANGES YOUR RUNWAY TO 36L

"YOU" TO CLOSE TO AIRCRAFT "Z"

YOUR FLIGHT PATH IF TOLD TO MAKE A RIGHT 360°

Diagram "S"

Chapter IV

Tower Separation Techniques

It is obvious that airplanes can't stop inflight. They can slow down, turn, descend, and climb, but they can't stop, so when aircraft get bunched together, the controller must use quick thinking to remedy the situation. I call these remedies "tower tricks".

Look at diagram S. Let's say air traffic control thinks you are following too close to aircraft Z. He might say, "Go around," meaning for you to <u>over fly</u> the runway and remain in the traffic pattern without landing. The reason a "Go around" is issued varies. For example, an aircraft is slow to take-off and has not yet left the runway, the tower might say, "Go around, parallel the runway to the right, and when speed and altitude permit, start a right turn to downwind." ATC doesn't want you to <u>over fly</u> the runway while another aircraft is taking-off on that runway. Instead, he tells you to parallel your flight path. With these instructions we hear the magic words, "...when speed and altitude permit...", a phrase designed to protect the controller should you exercise poor judgement, turn and spin in. Basically, he wants you on the downwind leg as soon as possible so he can issue you a new landing sequence. Another choice ATC has would be to assign you to another runway. ATC can increase your spacing with aircraft Z by assigning you a 360 degree turn. "Cessna three four Bravo make a right 360 for spacing." In executing this maneuver, be sure to watch your altitude *This reminds me of a time when I was coming into San*

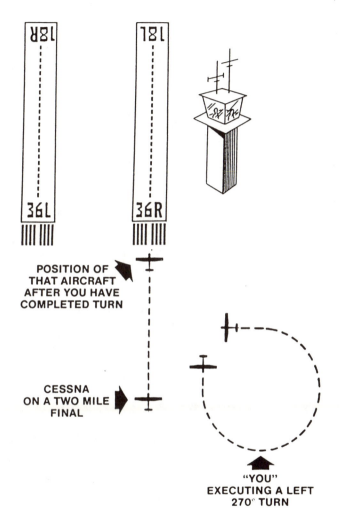

POSITION OF
THAT AIRCRAFT
AFTER YOU HAVE
COMPLETED TURN

CESSNA
ON A TWO MILE
FINAL

"YOU"
EXECUTING A LEFT
270° TURN

Diagram "T"

Francisco and heard that a TWA 707 was getting too close to a DC-9. Approach Control, seeing that no one was behind TWA said, "TWA 707, make a right 360 for spacing." The pilot responded, "What? Do you realize that it costs my company a hundred dollars for every 180 degree turn that I make in this thing?" A controller often waits years for the opportunity to slip in a zinger and he replied, "Roger, give me a two hundred dollar turn to the right."

One of the most popular spacing tricks the tower uses is the 270 degree turn. See diagram T. It is most commonly used when the tower wants to keep the downwind leg from being extended too far from the airport. Perhaps the visibility is poor or a neighboring airport is a few miles away and he doesn't want traffic to conflict with another airport traffic area.

ATC: "Cessna three four Bravo make a
                   left 270 and re-enter on base, num-
                   ber two following the Cessna on a
                   two mile final."

You: "Cessna three four Bravo."

Students often ask how quick of a turn to make, or how steep to bank. These are not questions that have a cut and dry answer. The pilot must make the determination himself depending on the speed and capability of the aircraft. All the tower wants you to do is to stay in your little area and to follow the aircraft on a two mile final. If, when you roll out on base and you end up still too close to your traffic, then the tower will send you around.

Spacing a straight-in approach when following another aircraft is not as easy as it may seem. Even the tower has a gread deal of difficulty judging how close you are getting

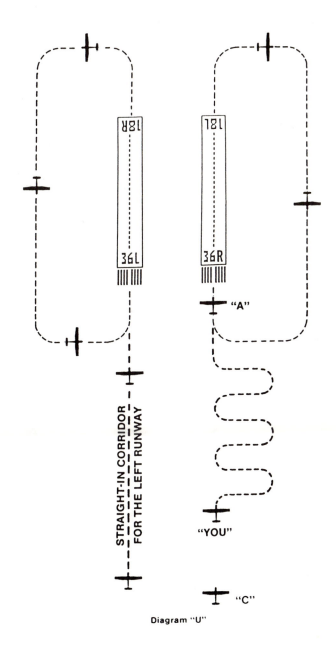

Diagram "U"

to another aircraft. It is your job as pilot in command to do the spacing as best you can so the tower doesn't have to. For example, let's say you are following aircraft A on a straight-in approach to runway 36R and because you are in a faster aircraft, you see that you are getting a little bit too close, as in diagram U. At this point, don't think the tower is necessarily going to give you any hints because he can always make you go around. For the purpose of this example, it is Saturday, and the left runway is too busy. You are being followed by aircraft C, also coming straight-in for the right runway. Slowing down to follow your traffic might come as a sudden surprise to aircraft C.

You: "Tower, Cessna three four Bravo will have to 'S' turn to follow my traffic."

Tower: "Cessna three four Bravo, 'S' turn to the right as necessary to follow your trafic, remain clear of the final for 36L."

You: "Three four Bravo."

By "S" turning you are buying time and therefore increasing the spacing between you and aircraft A. By recognizing the situation early enough, you give the tower adequate warning to tell aircraft C that you are "S" turning. This gives aircraft C the option of slowing down, "S" turning, or both. The tower told you to remain clear of the straight-in course for 36L because he doesn't want you close to the aircraft in left traffic.

Operation Lights On

The F.A.A. has encouraged aircraft to operate during the daytime with landing lights on when operating in and out of a terminal area. (Operation Lights On) It is a good idea because it helps other pilots to see and avoid you.

Birds also seem to avoid the lights and so it reduces the incidence of bird strikes.

Distance perception in humans is limited to about twenty feet of distance. Thereafter we judge greater distances by the relative size of objects. The smaller a Cessna 150 looks, the farther away it is, the bigger it looks, the closer it is. Sometimes the tower may be watching for you coming straight-in and only see your light. Consequently, to help judge your distance from the airport or other traffic, he may say, "Cessna three four Bravo turn off your landing light." You haven't done anything wrong by having your lights on, but you might assist him seeing you and approximating your distance for sequencing.

Split Frequencies

Split frequencies are common at many busy multiple runway airports. The tower has the capability of working traffic on two separate frequencies with two separate controllers each working a different runway. Unfortunately for the newcomer to a strange airport, he or she may not know that Local Control is split. The sectional charts only list the primary or major frequency available, and unless the other frequency is given on the ATIS, or you happen to carry an Airman's Information Manual with you, you won't know it. The tower will give you the other frequency after you initially call up for landing, if you are in a better position to use the other runway.

If you are taking-off from 36R but wish to fly left traffic and do touch-and-goes on the left runway, then the

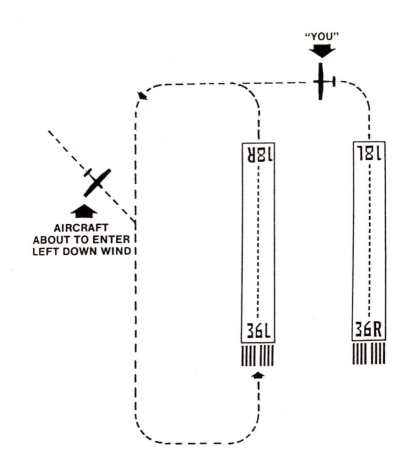

"YOU"

18R

18L

AIRCRAFT
ABOUT TO ENTER
LEFT DOWN WIND

36L

36R

Diagram "V"

controller might say, "Cleared for take-off, continue straight-out until advised." See diagram V. When it is safe for you to start your left crosswind turn he'll say, "...left turn approved, contact the tower now on 126.4." So you start your turn, change frequencies, and say, "Tower, Cessna three four Bravo's with you." He will probably say, "Roger three four Bravo, fly left traffic, watch for a Cessna about to enter left downwind." You then respond, "Roger, we have him."

The next chapter deals with how traffic is organized at airports without control towers.

Chapter V

Uncontrolled Fields

Basically, an uncontrolled field is any airport that does not have a control tower in operation. Included in this category are airports with a flight service station, unicom, or multicom. The F.A.A. has recommended safety practices rather than adopting strict regulations. There are good reasons for this. First, no two airports are exactly alike with respect to terrain differences, types and lengths of runways, and lighting. The terrain might be such that the only safe way to land and take-off might be to make a straight-in approach and a straight-out departure. Second, it would be difficult to enforce such regulations. The basic logic has been to recommend good operating practices and hope that as many pilots as possible follow the recommended procedures, and at the same time, keep pilots from being lulled into a false sense of security. Everyone flying is not following the recommendations. In other words, be on the look out for the guy who thinks he knows a better way than the one recommended. The F.A.A. recommends that VFR aircraft, entering an uncontrolled field, should not make any other kind of entry to the active runway except the standard 45 degree entry to the downwind leg. If everyone made straight-in and base leg entries without the help of a tower, it might compromise safety.

Tower Closed

If the airport control tower is not operating, the field, oddly enough is called uncontrolled.

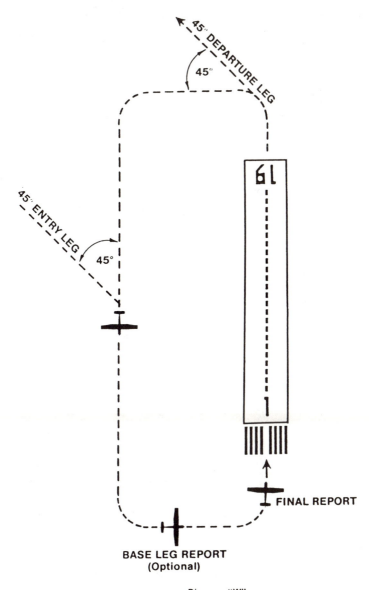

45° DEPARTURE LEG

45°

45° ENTRY LEG

45°

19

FINAL REPORT

BASE LEG REPORT
(Optional)

Diagram "W"

Let's examine a situation that deals with a control tower that is closed for the night. You want to know what the wind is, whether or not right or left traffic is in effect, etc. One idea might be to fly over the field. You should fly high enough to stay out of the possible traffic in the pattern, but low enough to clearly see the segmented circle and wind sock. The tower is closed so there is no airport traffic area. It would be a good idea to use 2000 feet AGL as your altitude as you take a peek at the airport conditions. Your altimeter will not be as accurate as if the tower gave you a current one, but if you have been keeping your altimeter updated as you fly, it should not be too far off. You might also hear other aircraft reporting **in the blind,** that will clue you as to what runways are in use. **Broadcasting in the blind** is a phrase meaning a one way communication. It allows other aircraft on the same frequency to hear your position and intentions. If everyone is monitoring the same frequency, it will certainly add to the safe, orderly movement of traffic entering and exiting the traffic patern.

When you are approaching the airport, tune in the tower frequency and listen to the activity. *(Remember, only an Air Traffic Controller can clear you to land or sequence you into the traffic pattern.)* Let's assume that you have figured out what runway is in use. You fly the 45 degree entry and as you turn downwind you say, "Buchanan traffic, Cessna three four Bravo, left downwind runway 1." See diagram W. Then as you turn final approach, you say, "Buchanan traffic, Cessna three four Bravo turning final, runway 1." Or even more specifically, "Buchanan traffic, Cessna three four Bravo turning a one mile final." You should always indicate your mileage if you are flying a larger than usual traffic pattern so that others don't lose sight of you. In addition, to help someone spacing themselves behind you, it might be helpful for you to include, "Buchanan traffic, Cessna three four Bravo turning a two mile final, full stop, "or "touch and go." If the pilot following you knows you are doing a full stop, he or she will give you more room because they know you will need time to slow down and turn off the runway. Conversely, if you are doing a touch-and-go, he will know that you will not need the extra time and will space himself accordingly. If the traffic pattern is busy, a base leg broadcast in the blind might be a good idea, "Buchanan traffic, Cessna three four Bravo turning left base, runway 1."

If you are parked at this airport and you wish to depart, you simply taxi out, look at the wind sock, pick the best runway and before you take the active runway, you broadcast in the blind on the primary tower frequency. "Buchanan traffic, Cessna three four Bravo departing runway 1." *Remember to depart on the standard 45 degree exit leg staying clear of arriving aircraft that are on the 45 degree entry leg.* Fly a reasonable distance before heading on course so as not to conflict with other inbound or outbound traffic. If you are departing but intend to remain in the traffic pattern then say, "Buchanan traffic, Cessna three four Bravo departing runway 1, remaining in the pattern," or "closed traffic." *As another general note, if the airport has parallel runways it may be the policy of the airport and the tower to only light one runway after the tower closes. Suppose the segmented circle indicates left traffic for the favored runway. If the wind favors runway 18R, the only lighted runway, then you would be flying left traffic for runway 18R as if the left and right designation did not exist. I just through that I would throw in a little mental gymnastics exercise!*

Flight Service Station

The next situation to cover is the field where there is no tower, but there is a flight service station. The flight service station has what is called an Airport Advisory Service. The frequency 123.6 is the one frequency assigned for traffic pattern reports. To ease congestion, flight plan position reports and weather briefings, should not be conducted on this frequency, only traffic information. The FSS personnel can not clear you to land or take-off. They can only advise you of other traffic. It is your responsibility to see and avoid other aircraft. When talking to a FSS, you call and say, "Ukiah radio," to say, "Ukiah flight service station" would be quite a mouthful. If you call, "Ukiah radio..." you are calling the flight service station on the field in Ukiah.

The flight service station may listen to many frequencies that are assigned to it, until you call. Then the flight service station specialist will push the transmission button on his radio for the frequency that you're on and talk to you. If you don't tell the flight service station which frequency you are monitoring, he often times has to guess. In addition, whenever talking to a flight service station, make an initial call up.

You:	"Ukiah radio, Cessna one two three four Bravo listening 123.6"
FSS:	"Cessna three four Bravo, Ukiah Radio."
You:	"Cessna three four Bravo transient parking, taxi for take-off VFR northbound."

FSS:	"Cessna three four Bravo, the wind is favoring runway 21, wind 200 at 15, altimeter 3031, two Cessnas shooting touch and goes and one Cherokee reported ten north for landing two minutes ago."

First, you establish radio contact, then you get the departure information including what aircraft are operating in the area and approximately where they are. After your run-up you taxi up to the runway, look for possible aircraft on final and broadcast in the blind on 123.6, "Ukiah traffic, Cessna three four Bravo departing runway 21." The flight service station may acknowledge this transmission but can not clear you for take-off. You must determine if it is safe to take-off or not. If you are landing at this airport, the F.A.A. recommends an initial call up about ten miles from the airport. *Ten miles is recommended because if jets take-off and land at this airport, they can be at 250 knots and cover ten miles in about two and a half minutes.*

You:	"Ukiah radio, Cessna one two three four Bravo, listening 123.6."
FSS:	"Cessna three four Bravo, Ukiah radio."
You:	"Cessna three four Bravo, ten north for landing advisory."
FSS:	"Cessna three four Bravo, wind is favoring runway 21, wind 200 at 15, altimeter 30.15, left traffic, no reported traffic."
You:	"Three four Bravo."

When you turn downwind, you broadcast in the blind, "Ukiah traffic, Cessna three four Bravo turning left downwind, runway 21." When you turn final, "Ukiah traffic, Cessna three four Bravo turning final, runway 21, full stop." Again, you do not get a clearance to land, perhaps only an acknowledgement from Ukiah radio. *A bit of caution is stated in the Airman's Information Manual, "Caution: all aircraft in the vicinity of an airport may not be in communication with the flight service station." "Caution: All aircraft may not be complying with the recommended blind broadcast procedure."*

Now let's review what we have just gone over before covering any new material.

1) If the tower is closed and there is no flight service station on the field, then you use the primary tower frequency at that airport and broadcast in the blind.

2) If there is no tower but there is a flight service station, use the 123.6 airport advisory frequency and get landing information from the flight service station.

Tower Closed - Flight Service Station Open

Now, what if the flight service station is open but the tower is closed? The F.A.A. recommends that you use the tower frequency. The flight service station will respond using AAS communication procedures. *This is the procedure unless the control tower is privately owned and operated. If this is the case, your sectional chart will have NFCT (non federal control tower) next to the primary tower frequency. In these few isolated cases you should use 123.6 AAS and communicate as if the tower didn't exist.* If the tower and the flight service station are closed then you should transmit in the blind on the tower frequency.

Unicom and Multicom

It is a fact that the great majority of airports in this country do not have control towers or flight service stations. These fields are uncontrolled. They can be broken down into two categories, those with **Unicom** and those with **Multicom.** Often, uncontrolled airports are thriving airports with flying schools and fuel vendors. The flying school or the fuel vendor will have a Unicom frequency assigned to the airport. Normally, Unicom frequencies are 122.7, 122.8, or 123.0. The congestion and widespread use of Unicom frequencies has caused a need for more frequencies to be added all the time. Be sure to check the sectional chart for the airport's Unicom frequency. Unicom procedures are similar to AAS but are less sophisticated. When you get close to the airport, tune in the appropriate Unicom frequency and listen. You will hear everybody and their brother on the frequency 122.8 because it is the most common Unicom frequency in use. They will all be broadcasting in the blind at their respective airports and you'll have to really listen to hear position reports at your airport. If the operator of the Unicom is not out fueling airplanes, washing airplanes or on a lunch break when you call up, he might be near his ground transceiver when you call. If a Unicom operator does respond to your call, the conversation may go something like this:

You: "Nuttree Unicom, Cessna one two three four Bravo, six west for landing advisory."

Unicom Operator: "Cessna calling Nuttree say again."

You:	"Cessna three four Bravo, five west for landing advisory, Nuttree."
Unicom Operator:	"Nutree landing runway 19, wind is from the south, left traffic, no reported traffic."
You:	"Three four Bravo."

It is very much like using AAS except these airports do not have the sophisticated wind and altimeter instruments to spruce up their advisory. You should broadcast in the blind when you enter downwind and when turning final as previously mentioned.

If you call up and don't get an answer don't sweat it, just over fly the airport, look at the segmented circle and enter downwind letting down in a safe and careful manner. Keep your transmissions brief because there are often a lot of people who want to talk, all using the same frequency, if not at your airport, then at other airports near by. *People who operate Unicoms can not clear you to land or take-off, they can only advise you of airport circumstances.*

If there is not even a Unicom frequency assigned at your destination airport you would then use the frequency 122.9 commonly called **Multicom.** Multicom is often called the pilot's party line because it is a frequency that is assigned for pilot to pilot communications. If you and another pilot friend take two aircraft out and go flying together and wish to speak to each other over the radio, you would use 122.9 the Multicom. This frequency is also used at airports that do not show a Unicom frequency on your sectional chart. At these airports there is no operator stationed at the field to give you landing advisories so you are on your own. Broadcast in the blind your position on downwind and final so that other pilots monitoring the frequency can keep track of your position in the traffic pattern.

There is a hierarchy of frequencies that, depending on the communications available at any airport, you should use. First choice is the tower, then the flight service station, if not available, then the Unicom and last the Multicom. I might also add that 123.0 and 122.95 which are usually reserved for airports with control towers might be used for calling a fuel truck to come over to your parking space, or to request the fixed base operator (FBO) to make a phone call for you, etc.

The Airman's Information Manual lists the following frequencies as designated Unicom frequencies:

122.700	Uncontrolled Airports
122.800	Uncontrolled Airports
123.0	Uncontrolled Airports
122.725	Private Airports not open to the public
122.750	Private Airports not open to the public and air to air communications
122.900	Multicom Frequency - airports with no tower, flight service station or Unicom
122.950	Airports with a control tower
122.975	High Altitude
123.050	Heliports
123.075	Heliports

The remaining chapters deal with increasingly sophisticated radio procedures. A commanding knowledge of transponder use is a necessary tool.

Chapter VI

The Transponder

The **transponder** has become an integral part of aviation. The transponder is a little black box that you might have in your aircraft that enables the controllers at the radar scope see you better. When the transponder is turned on, it sends out a signal saying, "here I am." If radar receives the signal, it sends back a reply that blinks the reply light on your transponder as if to say, "I see you." If your reply light is blinking, it is said that you are being interrogated by radar.

If you don't have a transponder, or if it isn't turned on, your target on the radar scope will appear as a little pollywog. Mountains, weather, and antennas etc., can protrude from the ground and stick up into the radar's view. This radar interference is known as ground clutter. Without a transponder, your blip can disappear into the ground clutter and make you invisible to the radar.

Your transponder is called a 4096 code transponder because there are 4,096 possible codes that can be put into the four little windows on the transponder. There are only a few codes that are standard, the rest are assigned by ATC. If you are assigned a **discreet code,** you and only you, are using it in your area on that day or that flight. When you dial a particular code in, your blip on the radar screen will become much larger and easier to see. Transponders have an OFF, STANDBY, ON, and LO SENS position. The STANDBY position is similar to what we might call a warmup position. Selecting LO SENS is a lower power adjustment that is very rarely used.

Many aircraft are coming equipped with **Mode C** altitude reporting. If your aircraft is so equipped, then your altimeter has been hooked up to the transponder. When told to **squawk,** ATC means turn the transponder on with the appropriate code dialed in the windows. When squawking with the Mode C on, not only does the controller at the radar scope see you, but he will also know your altitude within 100 feet of accuracy.The altitude reporting portion of the transponder usually is on a different on/off switch.

While working on your Airman's certificate, you will read a number of different text books. Don't get stumped when the text books say, "Having a 4096 code transponder responding to mode 3/A...". Civil aircraft transponders respond to what is called Mode A. Military aircraft transponders respond to Mode 3. In reality they are identical and for reasons unknown, the F.A.A. and the military use different terms. So, when text books come out and say, "Mode 3/A" they mean transponders with Mode 3 or Mode A. Most of the 4096 possible codes simply serve as your name tag for the computerized radar scope. A few standard codes, when squawked have a specific meaning. Here are the standard codes:

1200	I am VFR
7700	MAYDAY, I'm in BIG trouble.
7600	I have lost radio contact.
7500	I am being skyjacked.
4000	I am a military pilot flying in a restricted or warning area.
0000	Military interception operations, should NEVER be used by civil (general aviation) aircraft.

All aircraft operating VFR squawk 1200. If you are 12,500 feet MSL and 1200 feet AGL you must have Mode C turned on. This is particularly important because large transports in the region may be traveling well in excess of 250 knots and need timely notification to be vectored around targets that pop up on radar.

If you lose radio communications with ATC you can at least get ATC's attention by first squawking 7700 and then 7600. The former will set off buzzers and bells and the latter will explain your problem to him once you've gotten his attention. The phraseology used when operating the transponder is quite straight forward.

1) Squawk number — operate transponder on the designated code Mode 3/A (dial in the number given to you and turn the transponder to on)

2) Ident — engage the "Ident" feature (military I/P) (push the Ident button)

3) Squawk and Ident — Dial in the code and push the Ident button

4) Squawk Standby — Switch transponder from On to Standby position

   Squawk Normal — Switch Transponder to the On position

   Squawk Low — Turn transponder to the Lo Sens position

5) Squawk Altitude — Turn on the Mode C altitude reporting system

6) Stop Altitude Squawk — turn off Mode C

7) Stop Squawk (number) — turn off specific code (this is used for military)

8) Stop Squawk — Turn off transponder

9) Squawk MAYDAY — turn transponder to 7700

Page 68

It will probably be easier to understand this chapter if you sit and read this section in the airplane with the transponder in front of you. The transponder is a wonderful invention that has added a great deal of safety to modern day flying.

When I first entered the world of aviation as a student pilot, I needed take-offs and landings. I needed instruction in cross-country flying. I needed to learn airplane talk. What I didn't need was any more initials to decipher, (OBS, VOR, ATA, CZ, TPA). Well I'm here to tell you it never stops. Our next topic is the TCA.

Chapter VII

Terminal Control Areas

The terminal control area concept came about because too many aircraft were flying VFR in airspace often heavily saturated with IFR traffic. These aircraft without transponders had every right to fly in these areas according to the visual flight rules set forth in the FARs. In the name of safety, something had to be done. Development and implementation of the **terminal control area** became one of the more feasible ways to organize all these aircraft to insure the safest possible flight environment. TCAs are here to stay for at least the distant future, and it is my guess that there will be more to come as traffic increases throughout the 1990's and beyond. I think the reason that some pilots don't like the terminal control area is because they feel nervous when operating in them. Nervousness is caused by a lack of practice operating in the TCA. Budgetary restraints can limit the amount of exposure to TCA proceedures during training. These next few pages will prepare you for any exposure to the TCA you may receive.

First of all, terminal control areas come in two groups: group I, the busiest areas, and group II, the less busy areas. (All TCAs are located in heavy traffic areas.) They have names like San Francisco TCA and Las Vegas TCA and are specifically intended for the airport mentioned by name, even though there may be many busy airports in the area. If you are curious as to which airports are in group I or group II, consult your Airman's Information Manual or look at your sectional chart and see if a terminal control area is portrayed on your map. If so, buy a terminal control area chart and it will state whether it is a group I or group II. The differences between the group I and group II are slight so I will list what they have in common first, then show the differences.

1) You must be able to have two way communication with ATC on the frequencies that are on the TCA chart (132.95 requires a 720 channel radio, if you can only get 132.9 that's not going to cut it).

2) You must have a VOR or TACAN (military) receiver, except for helicopters.

3) You must have a 4096 code transponder, except for helicopters operating at or below 1,000 feet AGL under a Letter of Agreement.

4) If you are in a jet you have to fly inside the TCA at all times when operating to or from the primary airport (SFO, LAS etc.) unless authorized differently by ATC.

5) Regardless of the type of aircraft you are in, if you are underneath the floor of the TCA, your speed limit is 200 knots. This rule is to slow everybody down because aircraft not wishing to communicate with ATC will be flying under the TCA. Slower speeds will give pilots more time to see and avoid.

The differences between group I and group II:

1) Group I terminal control areas require that the pilot in command be at lest a private pilot (no students as pilot in command).

2) Group I terminal control areas require your transponder to have Mode C altitude reporting, but it is important to note that ATC may, at their disgression

waive the Mode C requirement if you request such a waiver to the ATC facility at least four hours before your flight time. If you are going to operate IFR from point A to point B and point C is the primary airport, ATC will waive the transponder requirement if you must pass through the TCA to get to airport B in a group II TCA.

The people at ATC are very nice and hard working, and it is not uncommon for them to help you out even if your transponder suddenly stops working.

Let's take a look at an example of radio work involving a TCA. Refering to diagram X, the TCA is a group I. You are a private pilot and have the required equipment on board. You are departing airport A and wish to fly direct to airport B at 6,500. Before you attempt this as an inexperienced pilot there are a few things you must plan and prepare. Plan where you are going and what you are going to say. As you prepare for this flight, consider a few of these pointers and use them in your next TCA flight planning.

It is recommended before you contact ATC, that you position yourself outside or under the TCA at a VFR check point shown on the TCA chart as a red golf flag. This may not always be possible because of weather. An alternative to flying over a VFR check point would be to give the controller your position in terms of azimuth and distance (ie. 20 southeast). Try to be as accurate as possible. Distance measuring equipment (DME) sure helps in this regard but unfortunately most light aircraft don't have it. Remember to always use the format: who you are, where you are, and what you want. Of utmost importance, an initial call up should be used. Even if the frequency is quiet, the pilot can not accurately evaluate controller workload. Depending upon his workload, the controller must decide whether VFR aircraft may be permitted to

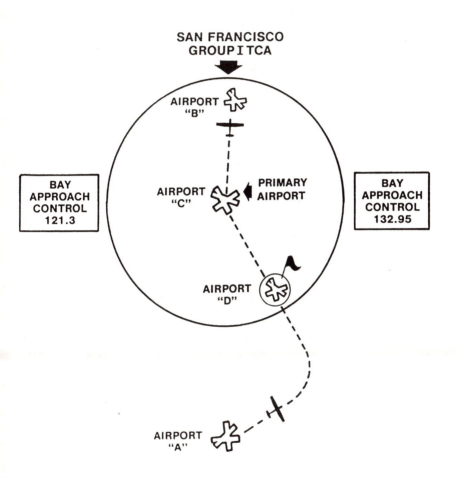

Diagram "X"

operate in the TCA. Radar services for IFR traffic take precedence over VFR traffic in the TCA. You should plan an alternate routing to your destination in case flight through the TCA cannot be approved.

Using diagram X for our TCA, you dial in Bay Approach Control on frequency 132.95. You have departed airport A and are level at 6500 MSL approaching airport D.

You:	"Bay Approach, Cessna one two three four Bravo."
Approach Control:	"Cessna three four Bravo, Bay Approach Control go ahead."
You:	"Cessna three four Bravo, two south of D, 6500, wish to go through TCA to B, I'm a Cessna 182 slant Uniform."
Approach Control:	"Cessna three four Bravo, squawk 4023 and Ident."
You:	(Say nothing and just dial in 4023 and push the Ident button).
Approach Control:	"Cessna three four Bravo, you're cleared to B via direct C, direct B at 6500, maintain VFR conditions at all times while in the TCA, traffic twelve o'clock, five miles westbound.."
You:	"Three four Bravo, roger and looking."

As you proceed, ATC will issue you traffic advisories. When you get close to airport B, if ATC has not handed you off to the tower you can say, "Cessna three four Bravo has B in sight, request frequency change to B tower."

ATC:	"Cessna three four Bravo, squawk 1200, frequency change approved, B tower 119.1, no traffic observed, good day."
You:	"Good day, three four Bravo."

You will now quickly change your transponder to code 1200 (VFR), change to 119.1 and contact B tower for landing. If B tower has an ATIS you might want to listen to it first. This is where two communications radios are handy, one on the tower, the other on ATIS. For those with only one transceiver, it is convenient when the ATIS is broadcast on the VOR frequency.

It is really not difficult to fly in terminal control areas if you anticipate ATC. Let's take the previous TCA journey and analyze the important elements. The initial contact went smoothly in our example, but ATC could have said, "Standby...", in that case you would have had to stay clear of the TCA until you had clearance to enter. Circling or flying any pattern that would keep you clear of the TCA would be satisfactory. *Pilots have received violations for penetrating the TCA without permission.* When you call ATC, it is important to be as brief as possible when describing where you are and what you want. If too much information is given, ATC will ask you to repeat the information missed and consequently you have more frequency congestion. Unnecessary chatter reduces the ATC system's ability to handle as many aircraft. Later in your transmission you described yourself as being a Cessna 182 slant Uniform. A Cessna 182 is the type of aircraft you are flying today, the slant followed by an alphabetic code tells ATC what type of specific equipment you have on board that might be useful to him. The following is a list of the slant (/) codes as explained in the Airman's Information Manual:

/X	no transponder
/T	transponder with no altitude encoding capabilities
/U	transponder with altitude encoding capabilities
/D	Distance measuring equipment (DME) but no transponder
/B	DME and transponder but no altitude encoding capabilities
/A	DME and transponder with altitude encoding capabilities
/M	TACAN only, no transponder
/N	TACAN only, and transponder with no altitude encoding capabilities
/P	TACAN only, and transponder with altitude encoding capabilities
/C	RNAV and transponder but with no altitude encoding capabilities
/R	RNAV and transponder with altitude encoding capabilities (Formerly called /F)
/W	RNAV but no transponder

(note: RNAV refers to airborne area navigation systems certified for flying RNAV routes in accordance with F.A.A. advisory circular AC 90-45A). At this time the suffixes C.F. and W are not generally added in radio talk, but rather are added in the written IFR plans so that ATC could utilize RNAV if necessary.

To continue with our TCA radio work, the next thing ATC did was to assign you a discreet code and ask you to Ident. ATC did not clear you to go direct B, but rather to "dog leg" a bit by flying from point D to point C and then to B. For reasons of traffic, this route was the safest and most expenditious for all concerned. When approaching airport B, he instructed you to go back to the VFR squawk 1200 and handed you off to the tower. In this example, you talked to only one controller all of the way to your destination, when in reality you would probably talk to several controllers on your way to airport B.

The whole ATC arena is like a big round pie with many sections called **sectors.** Each **sector** usually has one frequency assigned to it and is on one radar screen. When you leave one sector, or section of the pie, you will have to talk to another controller who controls that sector. These sectors are not shown on your charts but, the controller knows where he'll have to hand you off. The dialog will go something like this:

ATC: "Cessna three four Bravo, contact Bay now on 135.45, good day."

You: "Three four Bravo, 135.45, good day."

You change your frequency to 135.45 remembering to write down the last frequency 132.95. In case you are unable to establish radio contact with 135.45, you will want to go back to 132.95 and get another frequency. *If you forget to write down the old frequency and don't get an answer on 135.45 you are in trouble. If this does happen, then try 134.35 or 145.35 etc. in case you inverted the numbers.* If all goes well and 135.45 answers, continue:

You:	"Bay Approach, Cessna three four Bravo, level 6,500."
ATC:	"Cessna three four Bravo, radar contact, traffic passing 8,000 at twelve o'clock a DC-9 climbing to 15,000."
You:	"Three four Bravo, insight." or "...looking."

Radar controllers work in windowless buildings. They can not see the true weather situation. Operating VFR in the TCA means just that. It is your responsibility to maintain VFR conditions at all times. If ATC wishes to vector you (giving you headings to fly), it is your responsibility to tell ATC that to do so would make you unable to maintain VFR conditions.

ATC:	"Cessna three four Bravo, fly heading 250 vector for B."
You:	"Cessna three four Bravo unable due to weather, will need to go five south before heading westbound to maintain VFR."
ATC:	"Three four Bravo, unable due to traffic, can you go northbound around the weather?"
You:	"Affirmative."
ATC:	"Cessna three four Bravo, deviations around weather northbound approved, report when you are able to proceed west."
You:	"Three four Bravo."

There are many possible conversations but it is always best to use plain English to get your point across and to avoid confusion. It is possible for ATC to ask you to fly **hard altitudes** as IFR pilots do. For example, you might have to fly at 5,000 feet MSL or 6,000 feet MSL etc. If this happens, be very careful to listen for the instructions, "Resume appropriate altitudes." It means to climb or descend back to a VFR cruising altitude. Your response would be "Three four Bravo leaving six thousand for six thousand five hundred."

Now that we have discussed passing through the TCA, we need to cover operating out of a TCA like departing airport C and traveling to Airport A. Refer once again to diagram X. In this example, you listen to the ATIS and hear that the **Clearance Delivery** frequency is 118.0. To reduce frequency congestion, a separate frequency is provided to issue clearances. This position in the tower is called **Clearance Delivery** and is in addition to Local Control and Ground Control. You dial it in and start with an initial call up:

You:	"Clearance Delivery, Cessna one two three four Bravo."
ATC:	"Cessna three four Bravo, Clearance Delivery, go (or go ahead)."
You:	"Three four Bravo would like to go VFR to A at five thousand five hundred, I'm a Cessna 182 slant Uniform." (Get your pencil and paper ready.)
ATC:	"Cessna three four Bravo is cleared out of the TCA via after take-off fly heading 080 degrees maintain

VFR conditions at or below two thousand five hundred while in the TCA, contact Bay Departure 120.9, squawk 3223."

If you need time to digest all this say, "Three four Bravo, standby," then, when you are ready to read back the clearance, "Cessna three four Bravo ready for readback." This is not a requirement, incidentally, but it is certainly the wise thing to do. Depending on controller workload, ATC might say, "Standby," or "Three four Bravo go ahead with your readback." Then you readback the clearance exactly as it was given to you.

ATC:	"Three four Bravo contact Ground when ready to taxi, point niner." (meaning 121.9)
You:	"Three four Bravo."

Your transponder should be turned on as you are taking the runway for take-off and turned off as you turn off the runway to minimize cluttering the radar screen. After take-off the conversation continues:

Tower:	"Cessna three four Bravo, contact Bay Departure."
You:	"Three four Bravo."
You:	"Bay Departure, Cessna three four Bravo climbing VFR to maintain two thousand five hundred."
ATC:	"Cessna three four Bravo, radar contact, proceed direct A, I'll have a higher for you in ten miles." (Remember you originally wanted five thousand five hundred MSL and he

| | will let you have it as soon as possible.) |
| You: | "Three four Bravo." |

As you leave the TCA, the conversation continues:

| ATC: | "Cessna three four Bravo you are leaving the TCA, radar service terminated, squawk VFR, frequency change approved, good day." |
| You: | "Three four Bravo, good day." Change your transponder to 1200 and fly to your destination. |

Now isn't that simple? No? Well with a little practice and help from your instructor, you'll be an expert in no time. Remember to sound calm and don't yell over the roar of your engines.

Chapter VIII

The Control Zone

Our next topic is the relationship between the airport traffic area, the control zone, the weather, special VFR, and you the pilot. Many pilots still confuse the **Control Zone** with the airport traffic area. It is for this reason that I have delayed any discussion of the Control Zone until a clear understanding of the airport traffic area (ATA) has been attained. In review, the ATA is strictly for communications. You can't be in the ATA unless you communicate with the control tower.. The ATA is invisible on the map, and only is in effect when the tower is operating. When the tower is closed, the field is transformed into an uncontrolled field.

The Control Zone is depicted on your sectional chart or World Aeronautical Chart (WAC). Some Control Zones are effective 24 hours a day, some are part time. If a Control Zone is part time, the effective hours will be shown next to the Control Zone symbol. Part time Control Zones are usually in effect the same hours of operation as the tower or the flight service station on the field. For example, if the tower is open from 7 a.m. until 11 p.m., but the flight service station on the field is open 24 hours a day, then the Control Zone will probably be full time, even if the ATA closes at 11 p.m.

Unlike the ATA, the Control Zone will change it's size slightly depending on the airport it surrounds. The Control Zone usually has a radius of five statute miles with extensions as needed for IFR pilots entering or exiting the area. The Control Zone starts at the surface and goes up to 14,500 MSL. Why 14,500 MSL? In most parts of the USA at 14,500 MSL the Continental control area begins, which means that at 14, 500 MSL and above, all airspace is controlled. This has always been a source of confusion for some pilots who say, "I flew at 15,500 MSL and I didn't talk to anyone. Did I do something wrong?" All controlled airspace means is that if you're flying in the controlled airspace you must abide by VFR rules that are applied to controlled airspace. You can only be up there if you stay 1000 feet above the clouds or 1000 feet below the clouds. They must have five miles visibility and stay one mile horizontally away from the clouds. Following these minimums will help you and other pilots see and avoid each other. *These rules apply beginning at 10,000 MSL. (ref. FAR 91.105). Also at 15,500, as in the example, you would have to have a 4096 code transponder with Mode C turned on, since the transponder rule begins at 12,500 MSL.* If the Control Zone is out in the sticks, in the middle of uncontrolled airspace, then the Control Zone does not have a 14,500 foot ceiling but instead goes up forever.

The Control Zone was only established for the purpose of marginal weather. If it is a nice day, clear, and visibility unlimited, then the Control Zone is of no importance to the pilot. The Control Zone has it's own set of VFR minimums of 1000 foot ceiling and three miles visibility. If the Control Zone weather is at, or above these minimums, then the Control Zone's weather is said to be VFR. If the ceiling or visibility fall below these minimums, then the field is said to be below VFR minimums and only IFR aircraft may operate in and out of this field. However, the VFR pilot may use Special VFR procedures to enter or exit the Control Zone. *The rules for helicopters are a bit different than for fixed wing aircraft. We will only be dealing with fixed wing aircraft rules.*

Special VFR

First I will list the FAR's pertaining to special VFR and then explain the procedures associated with these rules.

1) Aircraft must operate while in the Control Zone with one mile flight and ground visibility.

2) Aircraft must remain clear of clouds while flying in the Control Zone.

3) A clearance by the control tower, flight service station or radar center must be obtained before entering, exiting, or passing through a Control Zone.

4) Control Zones which are modified by T's depicted on the chart do not allow Special VFR operations due to heavy IFR traffic. (These Control Zones are illustrated in diagram Y.)

5) No Special VFR operations from sunset to sunrise except if the pilot and the aircraft are IFR qualified.

6) ATC only provides separation of Special VFR and IFR aircraft within the Control Zone - once out you are on your own.

7) The controller may request that the pilot fly at or below a certain altitude while operating Special VFR in a Control Zone but the altitude specified will permit flight at or above the minimum safe altitude.

8) At locations with radar, flights may be vectored if necessary for control purposes or pilot request.

9) IFR aircraft have presidence over Special VFR aircraft.

Here is an example of how Special VFR works. Assume the Control Zone is below basic VFR minimums. You know from your weather briefing that the low visibility is a local condition and that if you can get out of the Control Zone, the weather will be much better. Rather than wait for the weather to improve, you elect to go out Special VFR. You

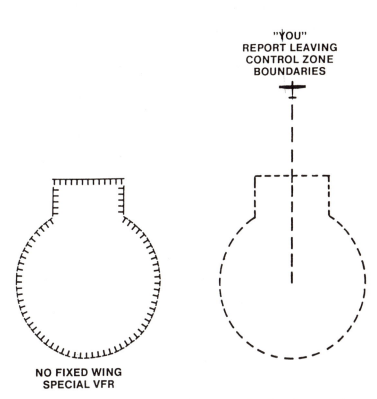

"YOU"
REPORT LEAVING
CONTROL ZONE
BOUNDARIES

NO FIXED WING
SPECIAL VFR

Diagram "Y"

listen to the ATIS, confirm the local weather, and then if there is a Clearance Delivery frequency, you use it, if not use Ground Control.

You:	"Buchanan Ground Control, Cessna one two three four Bravo."
Ground Control:	"Cessna three four Bravo, go ahead."
You:	"Cessna three four Bravo request Special VFR clearance to depart the Control Zone northbound."
Ground Control:	"Cessna three four Bravo, I have your clearance, advise when ready to copy."
You:	"Three four Bravo, go ahead."
Ground Control:	"Cessna three four Bravo is cleared out of the Control Zone north, maintain Special VFR conditions while in the Control Zone at or below two thousand and report clear of the Control Zone."
You:	"Roger, three four Bravo is cleared out of the Control Zone north, maintain Special VFR conditions while in the control Zone at or below two thousand and report clear."
Ground Control:	"Three four Bravo, clearance correct, advise when ready to taxi."

You:	"Three four Bravo ready to taxi with information Quebec."
Ground Control:	"Cessna three four Bravo taxi to runway 36L, hold short of 36R."
You:	"Three four Bravo."

Remember that to maintain Special VFR conditions while in the Control Zone, you must always have one mile visibility and remain clear of the clouds. When you are clear of the control Zone boundaries, say so:

You:	"Tower, Cessna three four Bravo is clear of the Control Zone."
Tower:	"Cessna three four Bravo, roger, frequency change approved, good day."

Only one aircraft at a time may operate in the Control Zone during Special VFR operations, therefore it is important that you report when you are clear of the Control Zone boundaries so other aircraft can depart or arrive.

O.K., now let's suppose that upon arriving home you find that your airport is below basic VFR minimums and you still wish to land. First, you can not enter the Control Zone until you get a clearance to do so. See diagram Z.

You:	"Buchanan tower, Cessna one two three four Bravo, seven south for landing with information Romeo, request Special VFR clearance."
Tower:	"Cessna three four Bravo you are number two, remain clear of the Control Zone, maintain VFR, I'll call you back."

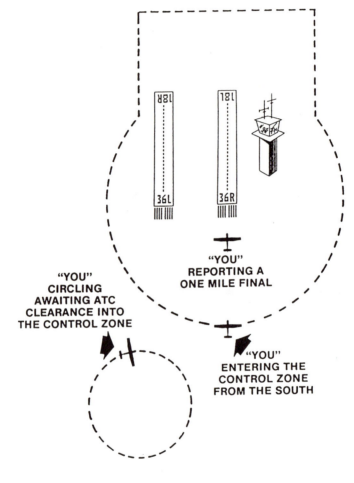

"YOU"
REPORTING A
ONE MILE FINAL

"YOU"
CIRCLING
AWAITING ATC
CLEARANCE INTO
THE CONTROL ZONE

"YOU"
ENTERING THE
CONTROL ZONE
FROM THE SOUTH

Diagram "Z"

You:	"Three four Bravo."

So you wait and circle. All the while making sure you have the minimum flight visibility and cloud clearance applicable to your altitude and location. Finally ATC gets back to you.

Tower:	"Cessna three four Bravo is cleared into the Control Zone from the south, maintain special VFR conditions at or below one thousand five hundred while in the Control Zone, plan straight-in runway 36R, report entering the Control Zone and report a one mile final."
You:	"Three four Bravo."

A full readback is not required, after all it is quite a mouthful, however, I caution you to make sure you understand the clearance and ask any questions you might have.

You:	"Cessna three four Bravo entering the Control Zone."
Tower:	"Three four Bravo, roger, report a one mile final 36R."
You:	"Three four Bravo."

You now proceed inbound and call again.

You:	"Three four Bravo, one mile for the right."
Tower:	"Three four Bravo, cleared to land."

Another word of caution, it is very difficult to fly a small, slow moving aircraft in one mile visibility and stay clear of the clouds. Even professionals hestitate to use the procedure except at airports that they are very familiar with both the landmarks and terrain. Be careful!

Chapter IX

Radar

Radar has become an integral part of VFR flying and the incorporation of radar over the years has become increasingly elaborate but not necessarily difficult to understand. Almost the entire United States now has radar coverage. Because radar is a line of sight transmission, it is limited to some terrain restraints and occasional weather distortions.

Radar assistance to VFR aircraft depends on a few conditions: 1) you must be able to communicate by aircraft radio with ATC, 2) you must be within radar coverage, 3) you must be able to be radar identified - a transponder sure helps, 4) the aircraft safety remains the pilot's responsibility. If the controller tells you to do something, and to do so would violate FAR's, (like fly into a cloud VFR), then it is your responsibility to advise ATC of weather conditions along your route of flight so that other plans can be made. If the ATC facility is unable to provide service on a particular day, it is possible that he is too busy with IFR aircraft. You should not question that ATC decision.

Stage Service

Radar assistance in the terminal area is called **Stage service.**
Note: "Pilot participation in Stage services is not mandatory but urged." (AIM) There used to be Stage I, Stage II and Stage III service. The Stage II and Stage III service

cover what used to be Stage I, now there is no longer a need for Stage I. Stage II and Stage III are similar. Stage II service provides the pilot entering or exiting the Terminal Radar Service Area (TRSA) with advisories of traffic and sequencing of aircraft into a smooth and orderly flow into and out of the traffic pattern. TRSA is basically the airspace that is controlled by either Approach or Departure Control. Stage III does all of the above, plus provides separation, by way of altitude and distance, for all participating VFR and IFR aircraft. The ATC standards of separation in this case are 1000 feet vertical separation between two IFR aircraft, and 500 feet vertical separation between two VFR aircraft or a VFR aircraft and an IFR aircraft, and a distance of one and one half miles or more depending on the type of aircraft being separated. Distance would vary, for example, between a jet and a Cherokee more than for just two Cessna 150 aircraft. It is still the pilot's responsibility to see and avoid other aircraft. Do not get a false sense of security just because you are on radar, radar is there only to help.

The Airman's Information Manual lists the frequencies that should be used when attempting to contact Approach Control, but, more commonly, pilots get radar frequencies from the ATIS. For example, the ATIS may say, "...Stage III proceedures are in effect, aircraft from the north contact Approach Control on 119.2, from the south 126.6, advise you have Delta."

When operating VFR and wishing to use Stage III service, Approach Control would like a little advance notice from the pilot. It is advised that you call up about 25 miles away so Approach Control has sufficient notice to coordinate your arrival with other aircraft in the TRSA.

You:	"Las Vegas Approach Control, Cessna one two three four Bravo."
Approach Control:	"Cessna three four Bravo squawk 4261, go ahead." (Here ATC is getting a jump on things by assigning a squawk. If you don't have a transponder just say, "Negative transponder or I'm a slant Xray.")
You:	"Twenty-five west landing Las Vegas with information Delta, I'm a Cessna 182 slant Uniform at 6,500, request Stage III service."
Approach Control:	"Cessna three four Bravo, Ident."
You:	You Ident but say nothing.
Approach Control:	"Cessna three four Bravo, radar contact, fly heading 080, descend and maintain 4,500, maintain VFR."
You:	"Three four Bravo leaving 6,500 for 4,500, heading 080."
Approach Control:	"Cessna three four Bravo you're number three following a King Air at twelve o'clock, five miles on a wide downwind for one niner right, report him in sight."
You:	"Three four Bravo, we have him (in sight)."
Approach Control:	"Three four Bravo, roger, follow the King Air to runway 19R, contact the tower on 119.9, good day."
You:	"Three four Bravo, good day."

Wind

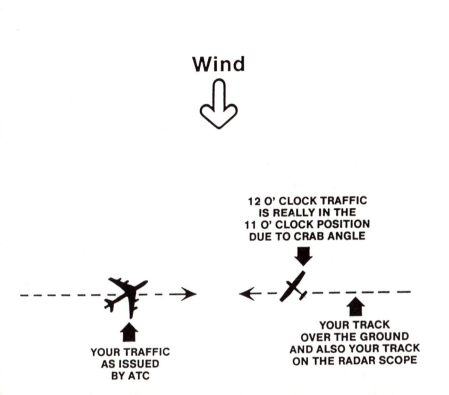

12 O' CLOCK TRAFFIC
IS REALLY IN THE
11 O' CLOCK POSITION
DUE TO CRAB ANGLE

YOUR TRACK
OVER THE GROUND
AND ALSO YOUR TRACK
ON THE RADAR SCOPE

YOUR TRAFFIC
AS ISSUED
BY ATC

Diagram "AA"

You:	"Las Vegas tower, Cessna three four Bravo's with you turning right downwind for the right."
Tower:	"Cessna three four Bravo, your traffic has changed to the left, cleared to land 19R."
You:	"Cleared to land, three four Bravo."

That is about all there is to it.

Traffic Advisories

There are a few things about traffic advisories to discuss. Traffic advisories are the same when given to you, the VFR pilot, as to an IFR pilot. The word "traffic" indicates a blip or target has shown up on the radar scope either expected or unexpected. The ATC controller may or may not be talking to this traffic. ATC will give the traffic position in relation to the face of a normal clock. Twelve o'clock is straight ahead, nine o'clock is off your left wing, three o'clock is off your right wing. This traffic information is issued to you in relation to your observed track on the radar scope. So, in a no wind situation, twelve o'clock will be right off the nose of the aircraft, but in a stiff crosswind situation, twelve o'clock could really be your eleven or ten o'clock position, as in diagram AA.

If you are given the distance your traffic is from you, it is in nautical miles. The direction your traffic is proceding is in terms of the eight points of the compass. If the controller knows the type of aircraft and the altitude, he will advise you. If not, you may get a transmission like this:

ATC: "Cessna three four Bravo, traffic two o'clock, four miles northeast bound, type and altitude unknown, Mode C readout indicates five thousand five hundred unverified."

The last statement tells you that your traffic is somebody he is not talking to, but the traffic does have a transponder with Mode C. Although the aircraft has Mode C, we cannot rely on his altitude squawk because the pilot of that aircraft has not verified his altitude with the controller. The controller tells you of the Mode C indication with the idea that chances are the Mode C is working and it is probably right.

Here are a couple of new terms, **primary radar** and **secondary radar.** Early radar was all primary radar. The scope would show many little polly-wog like targets transiting the scope. Weather and high terrain would poke up into the radar vision and obscure or create blind spots on the scope. Later, secondary radar came into being along with the transponder to eliminate some of these blind spots. During times of bad weather, ATC will sometimes switch to 100% secondary radar so that thunderstoms won't hinder the controller, and make him lose his traffic. If he does that, primary targets won't show up on the screen. The idea being that if the weather is bad no VFR pilots should be out there anyway! Sometimes the radar is partially down for repairs or maintenance. ATC may say on the air, "Primary radar out of service, traffic advisories available to transponder aircraft only."

Radar advisories come in many forms. If your aircraft is equipped with Mode C, a minimum safe altitude warning light may flash on his screen and he will say something like, "Cessna three four Bravo, I am getting a low altitude warning, check your altitude." You would reply, "Three four Bravo, I have the terrain in sight," or something to that effect, to keep the controller from worrying about you. Without Mode C this service would not be available to you.

You do not always have to request Stage II or Stage III service because by virtue of the fact that you have called Approach Control he will assume that is what you want. Don't forget to listen to the ATIS first. Nothing annoys ATC more than to have to give you the numbers when they are real busy. There is a lot of information that is included in the various advisories that are far too numerous to mention. With time and experience you'll see that most advisories you get will be quite straightforward.

Our next example will deal with departing an airport with Stage II or Stage III services. First, listen to the ATIS for the clearance frequency.

You: "Clearance, Cessna one two three four Bravo."

Clearance Delivery: "Cessna three four Bravo, go ahead."

You: "Three four Bravo request Stage III services northbound VFR to Reno, Cessna 182 slant Uniform."

Clearance Delivery: "Cessna three four Bravo, what is your requested cruising altitude?"

You: "Five thousand, five hundred."

Clearance Delivery: "Cessna three four Bravo is cleared out of the TCA, climb in VFR conditions while in the TRSA (pronounced tersa), maintain 5,500, after take-off fly runway heading, Departure Control 119.7, squawk 4131."

You should read back the clearance as given to you and contact Ground Control for taxi instructions. After take-off the tower will tell you when to contact Departure Control and when he hands you off to Departure, you change to 119.7 and say, "Las Vegas Departure Control, Cessna one two three four Bravo climbing VFR to maintain 5,500." Departure Control will answer with, "Cessna three four Bravo, radar contact, fly heading 310 vector for traffic." So, he says he sees you and wants you to fly 310 degrees so he can keep you away from other traffic.

Chapter X

VFR Flight Plan

This chapter explores the concept of the VFR flight plan and how it relates to communications. Suppose that you plan to fly a trip from A to E and will fly the route as depicted in the diagram BB. If you have trouble and never make it to E, no one will know that you are in trouble unless you file a flight plan. The best insurance of a quick search and rescue is the VFR flight plan. Time is the most critical element in your chances of survival, especially in remote areas. VFR flight plans are not mandatory, but recommended. First, let's see how a typical flight from A to E would go, and then use a hypothetical example of how it would work if you were forced to go down in a remote area and await rescue.

For our example, we have three flight service stations along our route of flight. I have called them Bob's, Jim's and Carol's flight service stations. You have called Bob's flight service station by telephone, received a weather briefing and **filed** your flight plan. Included in the flight plan information you have stated your estimated departure time. If after about one hour, if you have not called Bob's FSS by radio and **opened** your VFR flight plan, the FSS specialist at Bob's FSS will assume you have changed your mind and decided not to fly. Your flight plan will most likely be put in a stack of flight plans that are all over due to be opened. Your flight plan will sit in the flight service station for quite a while before it is discarded. The important thing to remember is, that if you are one hour or more late in opening your flight plan you need to advise the FSS when you initially open your flight plan so that your paperwork can be located.

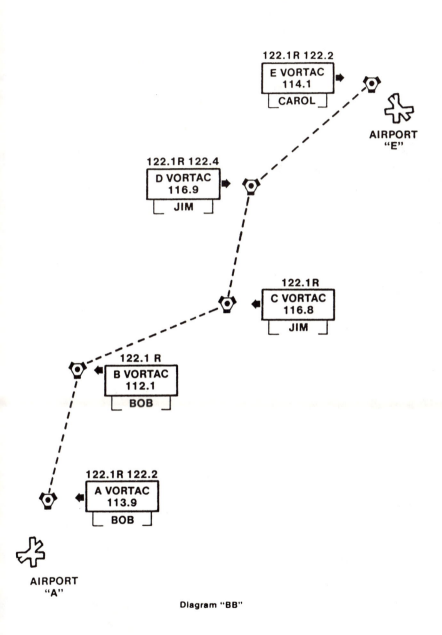

122.1R 122.2
E VORTAC
114.1
CAROL

AIRPORT
"E"

122.1R 122.4
D VORTAC
116.9
JIM

122.1R
C VORTAC
116.8
JIM

122.1 R
B VORTAC
112.1
BOB

122.1R 122.2
A VORTAC
113.9
BOB

AIRPORT
"A"

Diagram "BB"

Page 99

O.K., you take-off from A noting your approximate time of lift off and when time permits you call Bob's flight service station to open your flight plan. *On your sectional chart you will find the various frequencies available to contact flight service stations. In most cases the frequencies will be simplex, which means that you transmit and receive on the same frequency.* In this hypothetical situation in diagram BB, you can talk to Bob's FSS on one frequency (122.1) and listen on another (113.9). This procedure can be accomplished with one radio. You can transmit on the "Comm" side of your radio, and listen on the VOR side by turning up the Ident volume control. Looking at the A VOR box, it lists the frequency 122.1R. This means that Bob radio (FSS) receives (R) on 122.1 and transmits back to you through the VOR (113.9). If you choose to use 122.2, which is also listed here, you would transmit and receive on 122.2 (simplex). Here is how the radio work will go:

You: "Bob radio, Cessna one two three four Bravo listening on 122.2."

FSS: "Cessna three four Bravo, Bob radio."

You: "Please open my VFR flight plan from A to E at two zero."

FSS: "Roger, three four Bravo, we'll open your flight plan."

After that conversation, the FSS man will call Carol's FSS which is the closest to airport E, and relay all of the details of your flight plan. Now you arrive over B and call again:

You: "Bob radio, Cessna one two three four Bravo listening on the B VOR."

Page 100

FSS:	"Cessna three four Bravo, loud and clear, go ahead."
You:	"Cessna three four Bravo, I would like to make a position report on my VFR flight plan from A to E. I'm over B at three eight."
FSS:	"Three four Bravo, roger your position report, the B altimeter 3002."
You:	"Three four Bravo."

When giving time, all you need to do is state the minutes past the hour. It is understood that you are speaking of minutes past the present hour unless you state differently. Your conversation continues now that you are over C:

You:	"Jim radio, Cessna one two three four Bravo listening on the C VOR."
FSS:	"Cessna three four Bravo, Jim radio, go ahead."
You:	"Cessna three four Bravo, position report on my VFR flight plan from A to E, I'm over C. Also, extend my estimated time of arrival at E an additional three zero minutes."
FSS:	"Cessna three four Bravo, roger, the Jim altimeter 3010."
You:	"Three four Bravo."

Jim's FSS did not know anything about your VFR flight plan until you called. Only your departure and arrival flight service stations knew. However, after you call, Jim's FSS will call Carol's FSS and tell them to extend your estimated time of arrival an additional thirty minutes.

When you get over D you make another call to Jim radio giving your position as before. These **position reports** are not relayed to your destination unless you become over due and a search begins. Finally, you are approaching E and you call Carol's FSS.

You:	"Carol radio, Cessna one two three four Bravo listening on the E VOR."
FSS:	"Cessna three four Bravo, Carol radio, go ahead."
You:	"Cessna three four Bravo would like to cancel my VFR flight plan from A to E. I'm ten west of E."
FSS:	"Cessna three four Bravo, roger, your flight plan is cancelled."

You will read in text books to cancel your flight plan by telephone on the ground. I prefer to cancel in the air so I won't forget. Discuss this with your flight instructor.

Now let's say you are thirty minutes late on your stated arrival time at E. The FSS usually begins a radio search calling you on all available frequencies. If they receive no reply, they send out notices to all flight service stations along your stated route. In this case, Bob's FSS will notify Carol's FSS that you made a position report to them over B and Jim's FSS will say you called in over C and D with position reports. So when the Civil Air Patrol and everyone else starts looking for you they won't waste time looking for you along your entire route of flight, but will concentrate their efforts along the route from D to E until they find you. The information you have given on your written flight plan, especially details like true airspeed, altitude, and color of the aircraft will aid in the search.

A few words of advice on VFR flight plans: 1) don't file your flight plan in the air unless you absolutely have to because it ties up the frequency too long. 2) Don't attempt to open or close a flight plan with the tower because they have more important things to do. Occasionally they'll close it if they have time, (as a courtesy), but you should use the other methods that are available. 3) If you plan lengthy stops along the way, refile each leg rather than having one big flight plan. It is very easy to be inaccurate on your estimated time of arrival when you have several stops planned.

Chapter XI

Weather Briefings En Route

In flight weather briefings can be received in a variety of different ways. One of the newest and more popular methods is EFAS (En route flight advisory service), commonly called Flight Watch. The frequency is <u>not</u> used for position reports or the opening and closing of flight plans. It is strictly for gaining quick and easy weather updates and for pilots to make PIREPS (pilot reports) of turbulance etc. A flight service station designated as a Flight Watch station will usually cover a large area and have many ground transmitters and receives all over it's territory. Because there is only one frequency to listen to, 122.0, you don't need to state when frequency you're listening on, but you should include your approximate location so that the FSS specialist can select the transceiver nearest you.

You: "Oakland Flight Watch, Cessna one two three four Bravo, in the Red Bluff area."

FSS: "Cessna three four Bravo, loud and clear, go ahead."

You: "Yes sir, I'm en route VFR to Reno and would like the latest Reno weather."

FSS: "Cessna three four Bravo, Reno 1700 Zulu, clear, visibility 10, temperature 56 degrees, wind light and variable, altimeter 3001, over."

You: "Three four Bravo, out."

TWEB (transcribed weather broadcasts) are another way of getting an en route weather briefing. They are transmitted over the VOR and low frequency radio beacons and the broadcasts begin at fifteen minutes past each hour. If there is reason to have a special broadcast, it will be done randomly whenever it is deemed necessary. This is a one way conversation because these briefings are a taped broadcast. Remember that a normal radio call to the nearest flight service station will give you the needed weather information.

Chapter XII

Emergencies

Distress and urgency communications and procedures are extremely important and they need special attention in your home study. If you encounter a problem when flying, the fact that you will be under substantial stress complicates the problem. It is important to maintain a clear head.

Distress communications have absolute priority over all other communications and the word MAYDAY comands radio silence on the frequency in use. The word PAN indicates urgency and has priority over all transmissions except MAYDAY transmissions. Think of the word MAYDAY as meaning I am in big trouble now and PAN meaning if I don't get assistance soon I may have to change my call to MAYDAY.

You can obtain help from Air Route Traffic Control Centers, flight service stations, towers and Approach Control facilities. If your emergency happens when in direct communications with one of these above facilities, then just transmit the nature of your problem to them. If a problem arises and you are not in direct communication with ATC, you can call any of these facilities on their frequency or use the common emergency frequency 121.5 (243.0 military). There are several recommendations in obtaining emergency assistance and your flight instructor may have already told you of them. They are: Climb, Communicate, Confess, and Comply.

1) Climb - the more altitude you have the better your chances of being found on radar. The higher you are helps direction finding equipment, again because of improvement in line of sight communications.

2) Communicate and Confess - if you have a transponder squawk 7700 to start. Then communicate by beginning with "MAYDAY, MAYDAY, MAYDAY," or "PAN, PAN, PAN." Include in your transmission your aircraft number, nature of your distress or urgency, present weather conditions, your specific request, your present position or last known position if you are lost, your altitude or flight level, remaining fuel stated in hours and minutes, the number of Souls on board, and any other useful information.

3) Comply - do what you are told to do, however do not hesitate to tell ATC that you are unable to comply with certain instructions.

I will stick to the communications aspect of emergency procedures rather than delve into aircraft procedures because you should go into that subject in detail with your flight instructor.

In an emergency, do not worry if you can't remember all items that I mentioned under Communicate and Confess. If you forget any details, ATC will ask you what they need to know.

You:	(on 121.5) "MAYDAY, MAYDAY, MAYDAY, Cessna one two three four Bravo, calling any station."
ATC:	"Cessna one two three four Bravo, this is Oakland Center."
You:	"My engine is backfiring and I think it is going to quit."
ATC:	"Are you transponder equipped?"

You:	"Negative, I'm a Cessna 182 slant X-ray."
ATC:	"What is your position?"
You:	"I'm not sure, but somewhere between Sacramento and Fresno at six thousand five hundred."
ATC:	"Cessna three four Bravo for radar identification turn right heading 090 degrees."
You:	"Unable, I would fly into a cloud and I'm not IFR rated."
ATC:	"Can you turn left heading 180 degrees?"
You:	"Affirmative."
ATC:	"Roger, turn left heading 180 degrees and report steady on that heading."
You:	"Three four Bravo steady 180 degrees."
ATC:	"Three four Bravo, roger, turn right heading 270 degrees."
You:	"Three four Bravo right two seven zero."
ATC:	"Cessna three four Bravo, how many Souls on board?"
You:	"Two."
ATC:	"Roger, three four Bravo, radar contact, position twenty five miles north of Fresno airport, say your intentions."

You:	"I'd like a vector to Fresno."
ATC:	"Three four Bravo, roger, fly heading 195 for Fresno, Fresno weather VFR, wind 290 at 10, altimeter 3001, advise when you have the airport in sight at twelve o'clock, now six miles."
You:	"Three four Bravo, airport in sight."
ATC:	"Three four Bravo, contact the tower 118.2, they know of your situation."
You:	"Three four Bravo, thanks, good day."
ATC:	"Three four Bravo, good day."

Here was a typical example of a rescue by ATC and, as you can see, Three four Bravo had to be asked for most of the pertinent information because he was too wrapped up in his engine problem to remember all the details. It is no big deal, fly the airplane first, communicate second. Another example is the use of an urgency call such as in the following example.

You:	(on 121.5) "PAN, PAN, PAN, Cessna one two three four Bravo calling Center."
ATC:	"Cessna three four Bravo, this is Oakland Center, go ahead."
You:	"Yes sir, I'm lost. My last known position was near Lake Tahoe. I'm at 11,500 heading 100 degrees. I'm a Cessna 182 slant Tango, two Souls on board and one hour fuel remaining. Request a vector to Reno."

ATC:	"Cessna three four Bravo, roger, squawk 4231 and Ident."
You:	"Three four Bravo, 4231."
ATC:	"Three four Bravo, radar contact, 23 east of Lake Tahoe VOR, fly present heading for Reno."

ATC will tell you that the biggest problem they have with this type of rescue is that the pilot waits too long to call for help. He waits until he is running out of altitude, fuel and ideas all at the same time! Please keep that in mind.

The DF Steer

If you are somewhat lost, there is another method of finding out your position. You may be able to call for Direction Finding Guidance (Steer). On your sectional chart some airports with a flight service station on the field may also indicate that DF equipment is available. If so, it is an easy way to get help in reaching that airport or any other airport in the area. Students, in the course of their training may be introduced to DF by their instructors by requesting a practice DF Steer. DF equipment is not radar, but the ground equipment in the flight service station looks like a crude old type of radar. Actually, it is a radio receiver equipped with a directional sensing antenna used to take bearings on a radio transmitter. Your position is only portrayed as asimuth. Time and distance or triangulation are used to pinpoint your exact position. When you request a DF Steer, you will be asked to **key** your mike for intervals of five seconds. **Keying** your mike means to press down the microphone button without talking. When you key your mike, a single line projects from the DF equipment and a known direction from the station is determined. If you wish to be given headings to the airport, the FSS specialist will give you the reciprocal of your heading from the station. If the DF bearing shown is 100 degrees from the station, then the flight service station specialist will issue you the heading 280 to fly to the airport. Several times he will ask you to again key your mike. If he sees you drifting off a bit, he will issue you a corrective heading to compensate for wind.

A DF Steer is something you should try for yourself and it is a good idea to visit a flight service station that is equipped with DF to really see how it works and to understand it's limitations. Flight service specialists need practice once in a while too, so don't hesitate to try one.

The communications necessary to be issued a DF Steer are simple. Initially, start with the typical flight service station call up.

You:	"Sacramento radio, Cessna one two three four Bravo listening on 122.2."
FSS:	"Cessna three four Bravo, Sacramento radio, go ahead."
You:	"I would like a practice DF Steer."
FSS:	"Roger, Cessna three four Bravo, key your mike for 5 seconds."
You:	(you key your mike for five seconds, but say nothing)
FSS:	"Cessna three four Bravo, suggest heading 280 for Sacramento."
You:	"Three four Bravo heading 280."
FSS:	"Cessna three four Bravo key your mike again."
You:	(key your mike for 5 seconds)

FSS:	"Cessna three four Bravo looks like you have a little southerly wind, suggest heading 275 degrees now."
You:	"Three four Bravo heading 275 degrees."
FSS:	"Cessna three four Bravo, Red Bluff radio is also receiving you and we have your position as 15 miles east of Sacramento."
You:	"O.K. Sacramento, thanks for the practice, three four Bravo, good day."
FSS:	"Thank you for the practice, three four Bravo, good day."

Don't be a wise guy like the one I heard once who said,

Pilot:	"Sacramento radio, I would like a Lost and Found."
FSS:	"Are you lost?"
Pilot:	"No, but find me!"

Try to be professional, it is always the best policy. DF Steers can also be incorporated into simple IFR type let downs by utilizing simple turns and wings level descents. If the workload at the FSS permits, they are a lot of fun to do.

Skyjacking

Unfortunately, there is another type of emergency to be covered and that is skyjacking or air piracy. The pilot in command during a skyjacking is totally in charge and there is little that ATC can do. If you are skyjacked, it is important to notify ATC so that they can notify the authorities as well as follow your flight as it proceeds on radar. It might not always be possible to communicate your distress in detail so the best way is to squawk 7500. If you are already talking to ATC and he says, "Verify you are squawking 7500." If you say "Affirmative," or say nothing he will know you are being skyjacked. ATC will give you every bit of assistance that is possible.

Chapter XIII

VFR Flight Following

VFR flight following is getting to be a very popular way of travel. The disadvantages are that it is subject to the Air Traffic Controller's workload. When available, it is the best way to travel because radar issues advisories of converging traffic to you. Simply, radar is another set of eyes. In addition, if suddenly an emergency situation develops you will not need to scramble for a radar frequency because you already are on one. To request VFR flight following, it is recommended that you begin with an initial call up.

You:	"Los Angeles Center, Cessna one two three four Bravo."
ATC:	"Cessna three four Bravo, Los Angeles Center."
You:	"Over Bakersfield en route VFR to San Diego, request VFR flight following, I'm a Cessna 182 slant Uniform."
ATC:	"Cessna three four Bravo squawk 4237 and Ident."
ATC:	"Cessna three four Bravo, radar contact, three south of Bakersfield, verify 8,500."
You:	"Three four Bravo, level eight thousand five hundred."

ATC:	"Three four Bravo, roger, maintain VFR conditions, report any altitude changes, traffic two o'clock five miles westbound, no altitude."
You:	"Three four Bravo, looking."
ATC:	"Three four Bravo additional traffic eleven o'clock three miles opposite direction, Mode C indicates seven thousand five hundred unverified."
You:	"Three four Bravo, in sight, altitude looks about right."
ATC:	"Cessna three four Bravo, clear of the previously mentioned traffic, additional traffic, two, moving to three o'clock, ten miles northbound is an American 727 out of eight thousand for flight level two three zero."
You:	"Three four Bravo, in sight."

As the flight progresses, traffic will be issued on a workload permitting basis with IFR aircraft having priority. If you have to leave Center frequency to get ATIS because you have only one radio, advise ATC. He will say, "that is approved, report back on frequency." When you are back, say, "Cessna three four Bravo is back with you."

When you leave one controller's sector he might hand you off to the next controller and the conversation might sound like this:

"Cessna three four Bravo, leaving my airspace, squawk VFR for further flight following, contact L.A. Center on 135.4, good day." Here, ATC has not communicated with the next sector and when you switch to 135.4 you are going to have to repeat the entire flight following request to the new controller because the last controller did not have time to do it. The key to knowing this is that he had you change your squawk back to 1200. If he hands you off letting you keep the same discreet code, then the next controller knows you are coming and has agreed to continue your flight following. (Probably, because even though he's busy, your radio work is so good he finds it hard to turn down your request.)

Helping ATC

Receiving VFR flight following is not always a free lunch. During the course of your flight following ATC may request special assistance from you. Often times an emergency locator transmitter (ELT) will be sounding off at the ATC facility and the controller might need your assistance in tracking down the approximate position of a downed aircraft.

ATC: "Cessna three four Bravo, will you see if you can hear an ELT in your area?"

You: "Three four Bravo, standby."

You switch your number two radio to 121.5 and listen for the familiar siren sound of the ELT. If it is loud and clear then turn the volume very low until you can barely hear it. Then, if after the volume is turned down the ELT gets louder, you know you are approaching the downed aircraft. If the sound gets weaker, then you know that the aircraft is behind you. This information should be relayed immediately back to ATC. If you have one radio say, "Three four Bravo, roger, I'll be off frequency for a few moments." A great many downed aircraft have been found with just this kind of assistance from pilots.

Another way you might be called upon to help is by relaying ATC messages to another aircraft. Sometimes, due to the position and location of ATC's communication antennas, or any number of other reasons, a pilot has missed an ATC hand off. The pilot is now out of ATC's communication range and you might be called upon to help reestablish communications. *This would be a good time to have a pencil and paper handy!*

ATC:	"Cessna three four Bravo, Los Angeles Center."
You:	"Three four Bravo, go ahead."
ATC:	"Will you tell Bonanza two one Mike to Contact Los Angeles Center on 132.6."
You:	"Three four Bravo, roger, standby."
You:	"Bonanza two one Mike how do you hear?"
Bonanza:	"Bonanza two one Mike reads you loud and clear."
You:	"ATC advises you contact Los Angeles Center on 132.6, over."
Bonanza:	"Two one Mike, 132.6, thank you."
You:	"Center, two one Mike acknowledges and is switching."
ATC:	"Three four Bravo, roger, thank you."

The key here is to include the phrase, "ATC advises." This legally clarifies that your instructions are from ATC. Another simple request ATC might ask is a **radio check.** Perhaps ATC is having difficulty communicating with an aircraft and doesn't know whether the problem lies with the ATC equipment or the aircraft so he might say:

ATC:	"Cessna three four Bravo, radio check."
You:	"Three four Bravo, loud and clear." or "Three four Bravo, five by five." (means the same) or "Three four Bravo, you're breaking up." (in other words you would answer whatever the situation is).

ATC might ask for a **short count** instead of a radio check. He may even need a **long count**, which goes all of the way to ten and back. There may be some maintenance going on down there and they need a count of numbers to make the necessary adjustments.

ATC:	"Three four Bravo give me a short count."
You:	"Three four Bravo, roger, one two three four five four three two one."

Special assistance to ATC may come in the form of **PIREPS** which may or may not be solicited from ATC. A **PIREP** is a pilot weather report. You may advise ATC that you are encountering light to moderate turbulence. This message will be given to other aircraft in the area as, "light to moderate turbulence reported by a Cessna 182 forty miles ahead of you."

Windshear is something very critical that a pilot would want to report. Windshear results in either a sudden gain or sudden loss in airspeed and is critical on short final approach. In the future many large airports will have machines that will attempt to measure windshear. Until this equipment is available, ATC has to rely on pilot reports in order to relay the information to other pilots. When you encounter windshear on your final approach, you would give your report to Ground Control after landing. The report should include the altitude and the plus or minus factor of airspeed.

You:	"Ground, three four Bravo experienced windshear three hundred feet above the ground on short final resulting in a ten knot loss of airspeed."
ATC:	"Three four Bravo thank you." The tower will report this message to other aircraft landing at your airport.
ATC:	"Cherokee three two Tango cleared to land, wind two one zero at ten, windshear resulting in a loss of ten knots airspeed reported by a Cessna 182 three minutes ago."

Braking action on the runway is an important report that should be volunteered to ATC. The report should include which portion, if not all of the affected runway, is slippery (due to rain or snow). Terms such as good, fair, poor, and nil are most descriptive.

You:	"Ground, Cessna three four Bravo would like to report braking action poor, last half of runway."

Pilot reports of aircraft icing are extremely valuable and such reports will vary in length according to the experience of the pilot.

You:	"Cessna three four Bravo would like to report light icing at nine thousand in the clouds." Or, "Cessna three four Bravo would like to report moderate clear icing in rain showers VFR."

Icing reports are generally referred to as trace, light, moderate and severe. Turbulence reports are generally refered to in terms light, moderate, and severe, along with information as to how often you are encountering the turbulence, occasional, intermittant, or continuous. Weather reporting as a whole, depends on the pilot's ability to verbalize what he or she is encountering.

In the next chapter we will cover a number of topics that I call one-way communications. We will focus on pilot controlled lighting, no radio (NORDO), and partial communications failure procedures.

Chapter XIV

One Way Communications

Pilot Controlled Lighting

Aviation communications may include a one way conversation with a machine. An example of this would be pilot controlled airport lighting. Late at night when no one is on duty to operate the airport lighting system, some airports have the capability for the pilot to operate the lighting. This is accomplished by keying the microphone rapidly and transmitting clicks. Depending on the amount of clicks received in a five second interval, the machine operating the lighting will respond by adjusting the lighting accordingly. The frequency you use depends on where you are. If the field has a tower, you use the tower frequency. If just a Unicom, then use the Unicom. Generally, it is the same frequency that is used to broadcast your position in the blind.

When approaching the airport, click your microphone seven times in a five second period and the airport lighting will come on with the highest intensity lighting possible. The lights will remain on for fifteen minutes. If you wish to lower the intensity or to turn off the RIEL (runway end identifier lights) then you would click the mike five times in five seconds. If you wish the lowest intensity available, key your mike three times in five seconds. The level of sophistication of the ground equipment may be limited and you may not get the variety of lighting intensities available as you would if the tower was in operation.

No Radio

Another form of one way communication is the use of light signals from the control tower. Light gun signals are a crude method of communication developed to communicate with pilots of an aircraft with an inoperative radio. There are many disadvantages to this method, including the fact that the pilot might not be looking at the tower when the signal is given. In addition, the tower can only communicate approval and disapproval of what he is guessing you want. During the night, the only way you can acknowledge a light signal is to blink your landing lights. During daylight and while on the ground, the pilot can acknowledge the light signals by moving either the elevator or rudder several times. *Personally, I don't like the idea of departing anywhere without a radio, but if you must, keep a good sharp eye on the tower and look out for other aircraft.*

The types and combinations of light signals you might receive are listed in this book, as well as in the FAR's and in the Airman's Information Manual. It is recommended that you telephone the tower of your intentions before you taxi-out so they will expect you. If radio failure has occured en route, enter downwind and rock your wings until you get some response from the tower. You can then acknowledge the tower's subsequent light signals by rocking your wings. The Airman's Information Manual recommends that when approaching the field, you should initially fly the aircraft above the airport traffic area to observe what runways are in use.

Color and Type of Light Signal	On the Ground	In the Air
Steady Green	Cleared for take-off	Cleared to land
Flashing Green	Cleared to taxi	Return for landing
Steady Red	Stop	Give way to other aircraft and continue circling
Flashing Red	Taxi clear of the landing area, runway in use	Do not land, airport unsafe
Flashing White	Return to starting point on airport	No meaning in the air
Alternating Red and Green	General warning signal-exercise extreme caution	Same meaning as on the ground

Partial Communications Failure

Often times, your radio may only be partially broken. Skill as a pilot is in determining your problem. If your microphone fails you have transmitter failure but your receiver may work perfectly. On the other hand, your transmitter may be fine but your receiver is inoperative. If you are coming home from the practice area on Sunday afternoon and you dial in the tower frequency and hear nothing, yet you see many other aircraft in the traffic pattern, chances are it is your receiver that is inoperative. However, it could be just that particular frequency crystal in your radio. My suggestion would be to call Ground Control and get a radio check. If Ground Control reads you loud and clear tell them, "unable tower" and Ground

Control will bring you in. *I have heard many a pilot tie up the frequency for long periods of time trying to get the tower only to discover that his volume was turned down too far.* You might also check your microphone button. It might be stuck in the On position which would keep you from receiving anyone. If you cannot get the button unstuck, then you could unplug the microphone as necessary to communicate. Be sure to exercise all of your options before giving up!

This concludes the VFR section of this book. The next section is devoted to IFR communications but will contain information that is pertinant to all pilots and should be studied even if you are only a VFR pilot. After all, you are going to get an instrument rating some day, aren't you?

Chapter XV

Instrument Flight Commu

Flying instruments <u>well</u> is one of the most demanding and the most rewarding aspects of flying. There are many fine books on the market that deal with the subject of instrument flying. Reading this section alone would not be adequate preparation for an instrument rating but it will be one of the most important references you will need to prepare yourself. Once an instrument student learns how to fly his aircraft solely by reference to his instruments, thinking and communicating are the remaining two skills which must be mastered. Many instructors do not feel that sound thinking can be taught. I disagree. Sound thinking and good judgement depend on knowledge of the rules and options available to you. The best way to know what options are open to you in instrument flying is to gain a thorough understanding of the IFR system, rules and the related communications. IFR communications require cumulative knowledge. For example, asking for take-off clearance requires the knowledge of how to first call for taxi clearance.

I have broken down the IFR communications portion of this text into five parts: IFR airspace, clearance, departure, en route, and arrival procedures.

IFR Airspace

Almost the entire United States can be visible from some radar screen or screens. In most cases, the limiting factor might be altitude. Because radar works on a line of

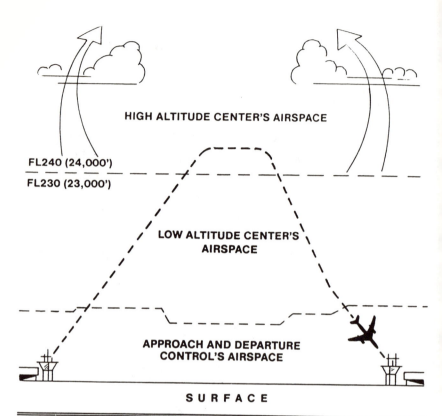

HIGH ALTITUDE CENTER'S AIRSPACE

FL240 (24,000')

FL230 (23,000')

LOW ALTITUDE CENTER'S
AIRSPACE

APPROACH AND DEPARTURE
CONTROL'S AIRSPACE

S U R F A C E

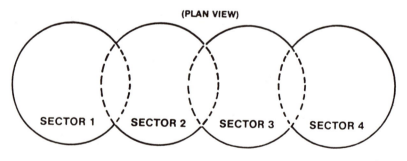

(PLAN VIEW)

SECTOR 1   SECTOR 2   SECTOR 3   SECTOR 4

Diagram "CC"

Page 126

sight concept, aircraft flying too low or too close to mountainous terrain may not be visible on radar. Whether or not you have a transponder will also be a factor in your being in radar contact for your entire flight. Severe weather or an occasional blind spot can also interfere with total radar coverage. We will discuss later what takes place when total radar contact is lost.

The best way to visualize the U.S. radar coverage is to imagine a pie cut into slices called **sectors.** Additionally, the pie is divided into three horizontal slices, from the surface up to altitudes that few aircraft are capable of attaining. Can you imagine one man sitting at a radar screen trying to keep track of all aircraft on his scope that are flying at altitudes from close to the ground all the way to 60,000 feet? Impossible! So, think of the horizontal slices of the pie as sections for the High Altitude Center, Low Altitude Center, and Approach Control. See diagram CC. The **Center** is a building with dozens of radar screens and air traffic controllers in it. Within the territory assigned to it, there are remote radar antennas that transmit their information back to the building. Along with these remotely located radar antennas are remote transmitters and receivers that also relay back to the facility. The Center primarily handles all IFR aircraft en route. The only time it also handles approaches and departures is when there is no approach and departure facility to govern the underlying airspace.

The Center is broken down into two sections, the High Altitude sector and the Low Altitude sector. The High Altitude sector begins at flight level 240 (24,000 feet) and continues up beyond flight level 600 (60,000 feet). The Low Altitude sector tops out at flight level 230 (23,000 feet) and goes down to the top of the Approach and Departure Control airspace. See diagram CC. Unlike the standard division between high and low altitude sectors, the division between the Center's airspace and the Approach Control's airspace varies everywhere you fly. The F.A.A. decides the division boundaries and is constantly changing these airspace boundaries in an attempt to streamline their operation, according to traffic demands. These boundaries are not our concern, because it is the job of the air traffic controller to hand us off to the next controller and to give us the appropriate frequency to do so.

A controller has airspace (territory) and is responsible for separating your IFR flight from all other IFR aircraft and from participating VFR aircraft while you are in his airspace. If you are flying on an IFR flight plan but you are in VFR conditions, you are still responsible to see and avoid other aircraft. Remember, radar can not see all the aircraft all of the time and the controller is not always talking to everyone he sees. Another important point is that a controller can not allow you to penetrate another controller's airspace IFR without handing you off or by getting special permission to penetrate from the controller that is in charge of that sector of airspace.

Below the Center's airspace usually lies Approach Control's airspace. If you are departing IFR then their name changes to Departure Control. Departure controllers are the same people as the Approach Control people and are both working in a different building than the people that work in the Center. It is not at all unlikely that the Center facility and the Approach Control facility are in different towns. The Center is primarily responsible for en route handling, the Approach Control facility takes care of arriving and departing IFR traffic as well as some VFR traffic operating in the terminal area. The Approach Control sectors are usually of smaller size because of the

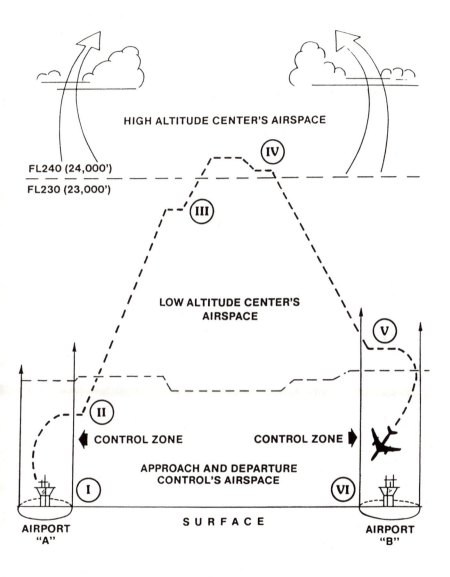

HIGH ALTITUDE CENTER'S AIRSPACE

FL240 (24,000')

FL230 (23,000')

IV

III

LOW ALTITUDE CENTER'S AIRSPACE

V

II

◀ CONTROL ZONE   CONTROL ZONE ▶

APPROACH AND DEPARTURE CONTROL'S AIRSPACE

I

VI

AIRPORT "A"

S U R F A C E

AIRPORT "B"

Diagram "DD"

Page 129

higher concentration of traffic in Approach Control's airspace. *Not many light aircraft are flying at 24,000 feet or higher. Most light aircraft fly at an altitude of less than 10,000 feet.*

The last division of territory concerns the Control Zone. If there is a control tower then the tower is in charge of it's Control Zone. If there is only a flight service station, then the flight service station is in charge. As mentioned in Chapter VIII, if the weather inside the Control Zone goes below basic VFR minimums (1000 foot ceiling, 3 miles visibility) then the field is said to be IFR and the Control Zone becomes effective. Clearance into and out of the Control Zone then becomes mandatory.

IFR Hand-off

Diagram DD illustrates in simplified form the normal series of ATC hand-offs on an IFR flight from A to B. Number I takes place as the tower hands you off to Departure Control. Number II is when Departure Control hands you off to the Low Altitude Center. Number III is the Low Altitude Center handing you off to the High Altitude Center. Number IV is when the High Altitude Center hands you back to the Low Altitude Center. Number V is the Low Altitude Center handing you off to the Approach Control facility. Number VI is Approach Control handing you off to the tower at the B airport. Since this book is geared more for the beginner, and not those who fly jets, few of the readers will need to be concerned with the High Altitude sector. I will not be differentiating between the high and low altitude sectors but will just refer to the Center to ease discussion.

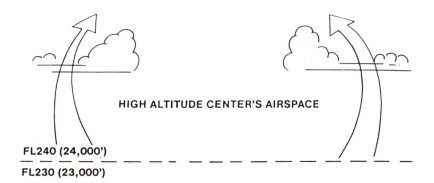

HIGH ALTITUDE CENTER'S AIRSPACE

FL240 (24,000')
FL230 (23,000')

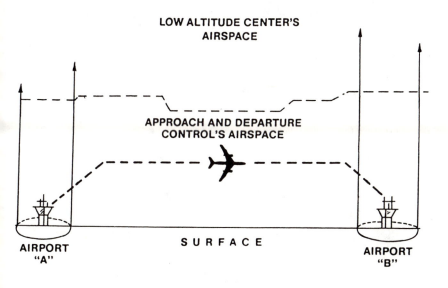

LOW ALTITUDE CENTER'S
AIRSPACE

APPROACH AND DEPARTURE
CONTROL'S AIRSPACE

SURFACE

AIRPORT
"A"

AIRPORT
"B"

Diagram "EE"

Page 131

The IFR Flight Plan and
The Tower En Route Clearance

The IFR flight plan is filed through your local flight service station, as is your VFR flight plan. The reason you must file your IFR flight plan is because you will be using the Center's airspace while you are en route. If you are planning on flying IFR from A to B as depicted in diagram EE, you would never get into Center's airspace. You would be in Approach and Departure Control's airspace the entire flight. In this case, you might not have to file an IFR flight plan with the flight service station. You would instead get a **Tower En Route** clearance issued by Clearance Delivery or Ground Control. The Tower En Route or tower to tower, as it is sometimes called, is a standard clearance from A to B usually with a predetermined standard altitude that has all been worked out in advance between the respective Approach and Departure Controls. In the past, Tower En Route clearances have been limited to IFR flights having destinations not too far away from your departure airport. However, the FAA is beginning to expand the Tower En Route portion of the ATC system and it will be possible to travel greater distances using only Approach Control facilities in the future. The plan is to publish standard Tower En Route routings throughout the ATC system and have the pilot file an IFR flight plan but to write TEC (Tower En Route Clearance) in the remarks area on the flight plan. The flight service station will route your flight plan via the Approach Control facility directly, bypassing the Center entirely.

Chapter XVI

The ATC Clearance

A clearance is permission to do something and this permission is granted by Air Traffic Control. A clearance is instructional in nature and contains several bits of information necessary to fly under instrument flight rules (IFR).

It is extremely important to understand that a clearance issued by ATC is predicated on known traffic and known physical airport conditions. To quote the Airman's Information Manual, "An ATC clearance means an authorization by ATC, for the purpose of preventing collision between known aircraft, for an aircraft to proceed under specified conditions within controlled airspace. It is not authorization for a pilot to deviate from any rule, regulation, or minimum altitude nor to conduct unsafe operation of his aircraft." In addition, FAR 91.3(a) states, "The pilot in command of an aircraft is directly responsible for, and is the final authority as to, the operation of that aircraft." If ATC tells you to do something, it is still your responsibility to make sure it is safe to do it. For instance, if you are assigned 9,000 feet as your altitude and the freezing level is at 7,000 feet, it is your responsibility to advise ATC that you wish another altitude to avoid airframe icing. If you are issued a heading to fly, but to do so might risk collision with another aircraft, you are expected not to turn and to tell ATC why in order that he may amend your clearance. Remember that traffic clearances provide standard separation only between IFR flights.

At airports with a tower, you will be issued your ATC clearance from **Clearance Delivery.** If the tower does not have a Clearance Delivery frequency, then Ground Control will issue the clearance. If you are operating at an airport with only a flight service station, the flight service station will issue it. If your airport is uncontrolled, you can get your clearance over the telephone with the flight service station. If you receive your clearance from the flight service station, a clearance prefix will be used. "ATC clears," "ATC advises," or "ATC requests," are the common prefixes used which let you know that the flight service station is relaying information to you from ATC. At uncontrolled airports, clearances will also contain a **clearance void time** such as, "clearance void after 2315 Zulu." This means that if you are not off by 2315 Zulu, then you may not enter controlled airspace IFR until given additional clearance to do so, which in most cases means refiling your IFR flight plan.

Essential Elements In A Clearance

Air Traffic Control clearances contain many pieces of information, the first is usually your **clearance limit.** The clearance limit is the farthest point to which you are cleared. Usually, the clearance limit is the airport that is your destination, but sometimes it is a fix somewhere in between. The fix could be a VOR or an intersection on an airway. Using a clearance limit other than the airport of destination is a method ATC uses to expedite your flight. Before you reach your clearance limit the ATC Center will give you further clearance and route you to your destination via the most expeditious route possible, given the traffic situation at the time. *If your radio becomes inoperative en route, you simply follow the IFR rules for lost communications after arriving at your clearance limit. We will cover this situation in Chapter 18.*

The second bit of information in a clearance will pertain to departure procedures. Departure procedures are issued to get you started on your way. They may not seem to be the most direct route for you, but they might be the established, orderly way to depart at your airport. Standard instrument departures (SID) are often used as a way of saving words over the radio. The SID depicts all turns and altitudes required to follow the departure routing. Departure procedures will often contain initial headings and altitudes to fly. *A few words of caution: know the terrain and obstacles that surround your departure airport. In the event of radio failure immediately after take-off, you want to confirm the failure as quickly as possible and fly the lost communications procedure spelled out in the SID. If you don't, the first heading you fly after take-off could be your last.*

The next information in your clearance will be pertaining to your route of flight. The route of flight information is most likely just what you had requested on your flight plan. However, it is not always identical. Traffic flow into and out of your airport or another airport close by may cause ATC to "change your filed routing."

Because of the need for more VORs in our expanding ATC system, the occasional use of split frequencies for VORs is used. For example, a VOR frequency might be 116.75. Your VOR equipment might not be able to receive that frequency. If your radio can not select 116.75 and a VOR on your changed routing has this split frequency, then you must advise ATC immediately so another fix can be assigned.

Altitude data is the next information that you receive in your clearance. Altitude information is extremely important. The words **climb and maintain** mean just that. If the altitude you requested is not the same as the altitude issued, ATC will usually tell you when you can expect further climb. You will be given a fix or set time after take-off when you can expect a higher altitude. This is important in planning your climb-out and also in case of loss of communications with ATC while IFR. The entire IFR ATC system is constantly subject to change during every-day use, but, it is structured so that in the event of a total communications failure, the pilot can still fly all the way to his destination in the clouds and not collide with another IFR aircraft. This is why it is so very important that you know all of the lost communication procedures by heart. ATC is expecting you to follow the procedures to the letter so that he can second guess your next steps and get everybody else out of the way.

Cruise clearances are few and far between and are usually only received for relatively short flights in un-congested areas. The term **cruise** used instead of **maintain** means that the pilot may climb to an assigned altitude and descend at the pilot's discretion without further clearance from ATC and make an approach at the destination.

Holding instructions are occasionally issued right with your initial clearance if you have been cleared to a clearance limit other than your destination airport. Hold-ing instructions are only for the purpose of getting you into a holding pattern awaiting further ATC clearance. If you experience lost communications and reach your clearance limit, you should follow your lost communications procedure. We will further cover holding patterns and their relation to lost communication procedures in Chapter 18.

The last two items of your clearance are the Departure Control frequency and the discreet transponder code assigned to you.

Clearances should never be left to memory – write them down. Your instructor will recommend various types of shorthand devised to consolidate the clearance information. A clearance is read rather rapidly, so don't be afraid to ask for the portions you missed to be repeated. "Say again the squawk." "Say again Departure Control frequency." "Say again everything after Cessna one two three four Bravo, I dropped my pencil." (An old joke.)

After receiving your clearance you should read it back to the controller. This is not an FAR but it is the wisest thing to do. You should not take-off IFR without making sure that you clearly understand the clearance. The readback serves as a double check for the pilot and controller. It is the best way to insure a safe flight by avoiding incorrect numbers and phrases that you thought you heard.

VFR Restrictions In IFR Flight

An ATC IFR clearance may contain VFR restrictions. The pilot must request the VFR restriction and understand that while operating on a VFR restriction, ATC will not maintain IFR separation. In essence, you are under VFR until reaching a specified point or altitude. Why would a pilot request a VFR climb then? First of all, it is extremely useful during instrument training. Procedures at some airports prohibit more than one aircraft to be in the Control Zone during an IFR approach because of the missed approach procedure. If it is a beautiful day out as you await departure for IFR training and another aircraft is coming in IFR, you have to wait on the ground until his "landing is assured" before you can be released. If you say, "We'll accept a VFR climb," then the controller can legally release you by saying, "Cessna three four Bravo climb in VFR conditions until three thousand, maintain seven thousand, cleared for take-off." This way you don't have to wait for the inbound IFR aircraft to land so long as you understand that you must maintain VFR flight conditions, in this case, until reaching three thousand feet, where at that point ATC assumes responsibility for IFR aircraft separation. VFR climbs can only be approved on VFR days of course, because if the field is really IFR then you have to sit and wait your turn. VFR climbs are also authorized to aircraft requesting them in order that a climb may be unrestricted. If you report the issued converging IFR traffic in sight, then ATC may issue an "unrestricted climb with reference to that aircraft." Aircraft look a lot closer together on radar than from the cockpit and what may be too close for legal IFR separation might be easy flying VFR.

Pre-flight Planning

Pre-flight planning is an art form in itself. I have seen pilots do an elaborate job of pre-flight planning for a flight less than one hour in duration. On the other hand, I have seen quick, brief, rule of thumb planning for a trip across the country. You should discuss this in length with your flight instructor.

How you fill in your flight plan is important. See diagram FF. First of all, your proposed time of departure must be accurate. If you are going to be one hour late in departing,

FLIGHT PLAN RECORD (FAA Use Only)

1. TYPE	2. AIRCRAFT IDENTIFICATION	3. AIRCRAFT TYPE SPECIAL EQUIPMENT	4. TRUE AIRSPEED	5. DEPARTURE POINT	6. DEPARTURE TIME (Z)		7. CRUISING ALTITUDE
					PROPOSED	ACTUAL	
VFR							
IFR							
DVFR			KTS				

8 ROUTE OF FLIGHT

9. DESTINATION (Name of airport and city)	10. EST. TIME EN ROUTE		11. REMARKS
	HOURS	MINUTES	

12. FUEL ON BOARD		13. ALTERNATE AIRPORT(S)	14. PILOT'S NAME, ADDRESS, TELEPHONE NUMBER, AND AIRCRAFT HOME BASE	15. NUMBER ABOARD
HOURS	MINUTES			

16 COLOR OF AIRCRAFT		WEATHER BRIEFING	SPECIALIST INITIALS	TIME STARTED		VNR
		STOPOVER FLIGHT PLAN				

FAA Form 7233–3 (12-79)   USE PREVIOUS EDITION

FLIGHT PLAN FORM

Diagram "FF"

call the flight service station and update your estimated time of departure or you will find yourself without a clearance. The ATC computer will cancel your IFR flight plan automatically if you do not request that your flight plan departure time be updated. Second, box #13, the alternate airport, should include the FAR required alternate. When Center gets your flight plan, only the items in boxes 2 through 11 are included. Box 11 is remarks. This is the place you would put such things as NO SIDS, NO STARS, or ADCUS (advise customs). Sometimes the remarks section is not handed off to each controller so if on arrival you are issued a STAR just say, "...request no STARS." NOT ("I told you people no STARS!!!") Be polite.

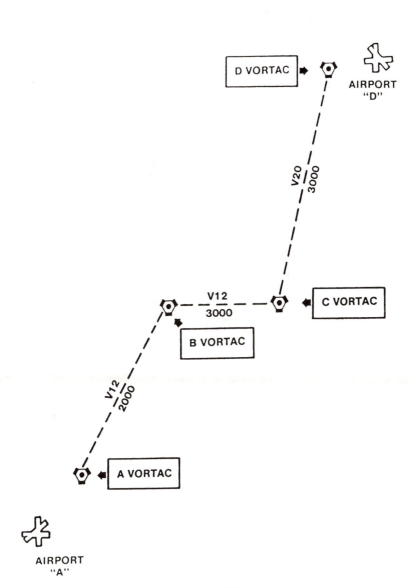

D VORTAC

AIRPORT "D"

V20 / 3000

V12 3000

C VORTAC

B VORTAC

V12 / 2000

A VORTAC

AIRPORT "A"

Diagram "GG"

Chapter XVII

IFR Departure Procedures

Imagine that we are at airport A (see diagram GG). Hypothetically, we have filed our flight plan from airport A to airport D. Our written filed flight plan has a route request of A V12 B direct D at 7,000 feet (mean sea level). We filed at least thirty minutes before departure so the paperwork will not slow up our departure. We look at our charts and find that airport A has a **clearance pre-taxi procedure, (CPT)**. Normally, we might copy our clearance in the run-up area but have elected to use CPT. CPT is not mandatory, but I can't see why anyone wouldn't want to use it. You can sit in your parking stall and copy your clearance even before you start engines. (Don't drain your battery down!!) At airports without clearance delivery or CPT, Ground Control will issue you your clearance. The phraseology is the same whether you use Ground Control or Clearance Delivery. Let's try a few clearance situations:

You:	"Clearance, Cessna one two three four Bravo IFR to D with information Charlie."
CPT:	"Cessna three four Bravo standby, clearance on request."

You could also have said, "Center filed to D," because maybe there is a way of going Tower En Route to D. This will alert Clearance Delivery to call Center rather than Departure Control for your clearance. Stating that you have ATIS information Charlie let's him mark your strip for their records. In this case, Clearance Delivery did not have your paperwork. At sophisticated airports, a computer in the tower sends a hard copy (written) to the tower automatically about ten minutes before your proposed departure time. That is why the Airman's Information Manual recommends calling Clearance Delivery no more than ten minutes before departure. If you call earlier, don't worry, all he has to do is pick up the phone or punch a few buttons on his machine and your clearance will be right there. The words "clearance on request" mean he is picking up the phone and calling Center for your clearance. When you are Center filed, your type of aircraft and type of equipment (DME, transponder, etc.) have been stated on your flight plan form and do not have to be repeated to Clearance Delivery. On the other hand, if you are going Tower En Route and did not file with Center then you must say, "Clearance, Cessna one two three four Bravo request Tower En Route to D, I'm a Cessna 182 slant Uniform with information Charlie." When there is no Clearance Delivery or CPT we use Ground Control.

You:	"Ground, Cessna one two three four Bravo taxi for take-off with information Charlie, Center filed to D."
ATC:	"Cessna three four Bravo taxi to runway 36R, clearance on request."
You:	"Three four Bravo."

As you are taxiing towards the run-up area Ground Control says, "Cessna three four Bravo I have your clearance, advise when ready to copy."

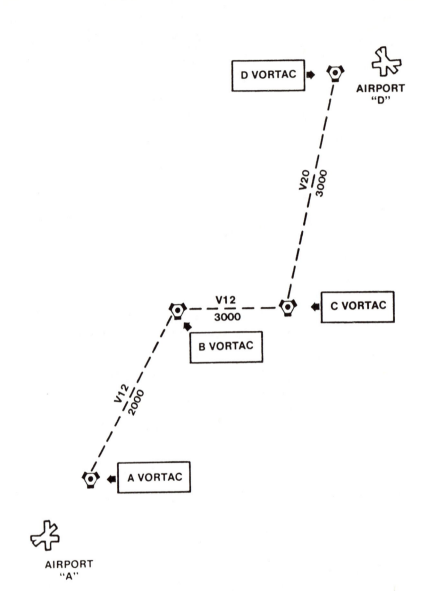

Diagram "GG"

You:	"Roger, standby, I'll copy in the run-up area." (A smart answer because it is hard to copy a clearance and taxi at the same time.)

After your run-up the conversation continues.

You:	"Cessna three four Bravo ready to copy."
ATC:	"Cessna one two three four Bravo is cleared to D, via fly runway heading, radar vector B, as filed, climb and maintain five thousand, expect niner thousand at B, Departure 119.2 squawk 4227."

If you need time to look over your clearance then say, "Cessna three four Bravo, standby." After you have looked things over and are ready to readback your clearance say, "Cessna three four Bravo ready for readback." He may say, "Standby" to you because if he is Ground Control, his first duty is to take care of aircraft taxiing. When Ground is ready to listen he'll say, "Cessna three four Bravo go ahead with your readback." *Using the initial call procedure when there is a break in the conversation allows Ground Control the ability to control taxiing traffic and wear the Clearance Delivery hat both at the same time.*

If you get your clearance through Clearance Delivery, don't be too concerned about the initial call before your readback unless there is clearance activity for other aircraft in progress. This is not written law, but common courtesy. Occasionally, you can shorten the readback slightly so long as the meaning doesn't change. Most often the readback should be the same phrases you were given.

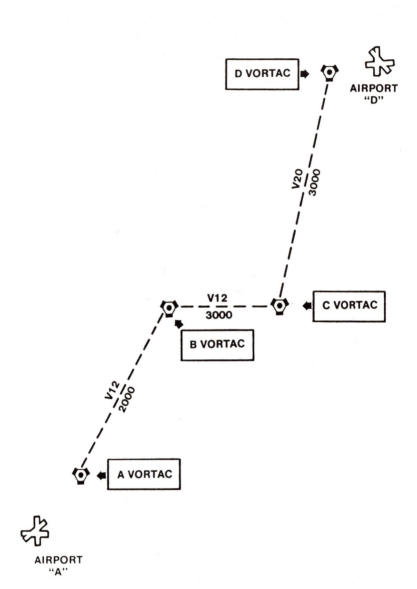

D VORTAC

AIRPORT "D"

V20 / 3000

V12 / 3000

C VORTAC

B VORTAC

V12 / 2000

A VORTAC

AIRPORT "A"

Diagram "GG"

You:	"Runway heading vector to B as filed, five thousand, expect niner thousand at B, one one niner point two, squawk four two two seven, three four Bravo."
ATC:	"Three four Bravo clearance correct."

What does this clearance mean? First, ATC wants you to take-off and fly the runway heading (runway 36 - heading 360 degrees) and climb to 5,000 feet. The initial heading of 360 degrees is the first heading in a possible series of headings that are intended to get you to the B vortac. At B vortac you can expect to climb to 9,000 feet, but cannot do so until further clearance is received unless you have a radio communications failure. The phrase "as filed" indicates that the route you filed on your flight plan will be followed. How did we file? The B vortac direct to D vortac, direct to D airport. Refer to diagram GG. So we are cleared by radar vectoring to the B vortac, then by our own navigation to the D vortac. Even though we originally filed A V12 B, ATC could not approve it and prefered to use radar vectoring to get us out of the terminal area. The Departure Control frequency and the squawk are self explanitory. Let's try another clearance.

ATC:	"Cessna three four Bravo cleared as filed, fly runway heading, cross B at five thousand to maintain niner thousand, Departure Control one niner point two, squawk four two two seven."

Here we are cleared as we filed on the flight plan, except, they still want us to fly runway heading after take-off rather than immediately flying an intercept head-

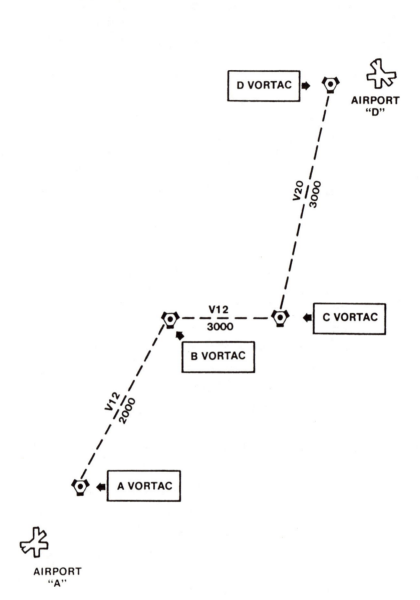

Diagram "GG"

Page 148

ing for V12. *If you experience lost communications then you would fly to the airway under your own navigation.* While in direct communications with Departure Control you follow the assigned headings (vectors).

In the clearance just issued, we were given **crossing restrictions.** We were told to climb to nine thousand, but to climb no higher than five thousand until reaching the B vortac.

What if you get an "as filed" clearance and for some reason you forget how you filed it! You wouldn't be the first person to do this. Just say, "Three four Bravo would like a full readout." ATC would then read your entire route of flight. If you ask for a full readout it may take him a while because usually an "as filed" clearance comes to him the way he reads it to you. He will have to call Center back and request a full readout from them before he can read it to you. A full readout is also called a "full route clearance." Here is another possible clearance.

ATC: "Cessna three four Bravo is cleared
                        as filed to D, except after B, V12 C,
                        V20 D, direct, maintain niner thou-
                        sand, Departure one one niner
                        point two, squawk four two two
                        seven."

He is telling you that you are cleared as filed, except you cannot go B direct D, but instead must fly V12C, V20D, then direct to the airport.

Remember, a "cleared as filed" clearance does not mean clearance for the <u>altitude</u> that you filed, <u>only the routing</u>. Altitude will be given in the clearance. If "expect filed altitude ten minutes after departure" is issued, then yes, you can expect your filed altitude. Again, these procedures were established to protect the pilot in the event he experiences lost communications.

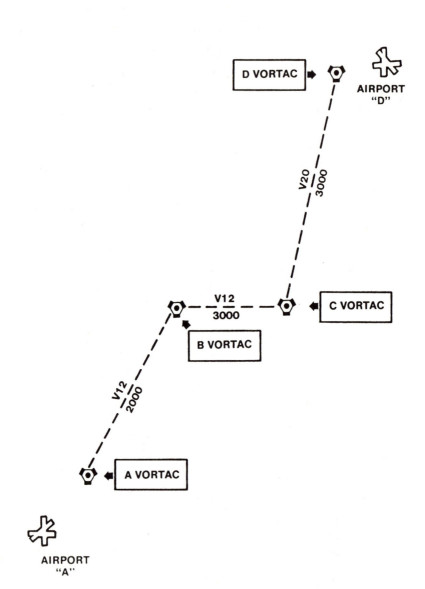

D VORTAC

AIRPORT
"D"

V20
3000

V12
3000

C VORTAC

B VORTAC

V12
2000

A VORTAC

AIRPORT
"A"

Diagram "GG"

Page 150

Clearances often times include **Standard Instrument Departure (SID)** procedures. The Departure Control frequency will not be issued in the clearance unless ATC wishes to change the charted frequency. In addition, the SID may contain crossing restrictions and this restriction will not be mentioned again in the clearance.

Standard Instrument Departures are published with minimum climb rates spoken of in terms of feet per mile. Not all pilots can comply with some SIDs because their aircraft just doesn't have the performance. It is up to the pilot to advise ATC that they "are unable to comply with the SID climb requirement." Once notified, ATC will come up with another departure and issue it to you. The reasons for the climb restrictions may not be terrain or obstacles, but for noise abatement or traffic flow during rush hours. In such cases you may be issued, "fly the SID routing, cross ten south at or above two thousand." What ATC has done here is said O.K., fly the SID as depicted, forget the published crossing altitudes and so long as you can cross ten miles south of the airport at or above two thousand feet, then you'll be able to clear the terrain easily within the parameters set down by the F.A.A.

"Fly runway heading" is a common phrase in a IFR clearance and ATC rarely states the reason why. The Airman's Information Manual answers the question very well. "Pilots operating in a radar environment are expected to associate departure headings with vectors to their planned route of flight." If a vector is issued after you have been established on your route of flight under your own navigation, the reason for the vector will be given. For example, "Cessna three four Bravo fly heading three four zero, vector around traffic."

Instrument students experience an excitement level in the course of their training that is difficult to describe. The anticipation of flying through real clouds often distracts the pilot from the business at hand. Consequently, the student overlooks some of the basics and prematurely calls the tower ready for take-off.When you have your clearance, and have looked over the routing, and you have done your run-up and set your radios...You are ready!!!

You: "Tower, Cessna three four Bravo ready for take-off on the right, IFR." (It is important to say IFR because he might clear you for take-off thinking you are departing VFR.)

ATC: "Cessna three four Bravo, tower, hold for Departure Control release."

You: "Three four Bravo."

"Hold for Departure Control release" means wait a minute, so that a call can be made to Departure Control to see if they are ready to accept you into the system. The tower tells Departure Control that "Three four Bravo is ready IFR to D." When Departure Control says "he's released," then the tower will release you into the IFR system.

ATC: "Cessna three four Bravo cleared for take-off."

You: "Three four Bravo," or "Three four Bravo rolling," or "Three four Bravo cleared for take-off."

After take-off, wait for the tower to hand you off to Departure Control. Sometimes the tower can forget you and if you think that this has happened, say questioningly, "Three four Bravo to Departure?"

Page 152

ATC:	"Three four Bravo contact Departure."
You:	"Three four Bravo." Then you change to 119.2.
You:	"Departure, Cessna one two three four Bravo climbing to niner thousand with the restrictions." (Assume we got the cross B at 5,000 clearance.)
ATC:	"Cessna three four Bravo, radar contact, delete the restrictions, climb unrestricted to niner thousand."

It is not uncommon for ATC to cancel crossing restrictions after all of your planning. The key element in this dialog is that you don't have to comply with the restrictions of climb and that you <u>are</u> in radar contact. Because you are in radar contact, you don't have to make all those position reports that are required by the FARs when operating in a non-radar environment.

You could dress up your first contact with Departure Control by adding the altitude that you are climbing through. This is especially important if your transponder has Mode C. It serves as a verification that your Mode C is working properly and can be reliably used by ATC.

You:	"Departure Control, Cessna one two three four Bravo climbing to niner thousand with the restrictions, passing one thousand two hundred."

This sounds very professional. If you forget, ATC will say, "Cessna three four Bravo verify altitude passing."

You:	"Three four Bravo, one thousand four hundred."
ATC:	"Altitude checks," or "Three four Bravo turn off your Mode C, I'm showing 8,500 feet." (Better get it fixed.)

Now that you've made your initial call and are still flying the runway heading, the dialog continues.

ATC:	"Cessna three four Bravo turn right heading zero two zero vector for B and traffic."

He has told you that he wants you to fly heading 020 and that this vector will be for two purposes. First, to get you headed roughly in the direction of B vortac. Second, to steer you around some traffic. Later, he may want to point the traffic out to you.

Now you tune in the B vortac, identify it, and check how close the issued heading is to the OBS (omni bearing selector) heading to the B vortac. You could then say, "Cessna three four Bravo's receiving B (vortac) suitable for navigation." "Suitable" infers a good VOR ident signal as well as a steady needle indication.

ATC:	"Cessna three four Bravo maintain the zero two zero heading, I'll have a direct for you in five miles, traffic is a Queenair, ten o'clock, two miles at eight thousand."

You:	"Three four Bravo, in sight."
ATC:	"Cessna three four Bravo maintain visual with the Queenair, cleared direct B."
ATC:	"Queenair one Romeo Whiskey, traffic is a Cessna 182, ten o'clock and two miles, proceding direct B, he'll maintain visual separation with you."

The main point here is to listen for the key words. "Heading 020 degrees vector for B" is not the same as "Heading 020 degrees vector for B <u>direct when able</u>."

Chapter XVIII

En Route Procedures

This chapter examines the radio work associated with the en route portion of an IFR flight. We will also touch upon flight through restricted areas, introduce you to the holding pattern, and discuss lost communication procedures.

Approach Control watches your blip on the scope and observes you are about to leave his airspace. It is time for a hand off to Center.

ATC:	"Cessna three four Bravo contact Oakland Center on one two zero point two, good day."
You:	"One two zero point two, three four Bravo, good day."
You:	"Oakland Center Cessna three four Bravo climbing to niner thousand passing through eight thousand two hundred."
ATC:	"Cessna three four Bravo, Oakland Center, roger."

ATC does not have to repeat "radar contact" and the pilot should assume he is still in radar contact. Let's say you tune in 120.2 and call Center, but get no answer. then you go back to your last frequency, 119.2 and advise ATC.

You:	"Departure, Cessna three four Bravo."
ATC:	"Three four Bravo, go."

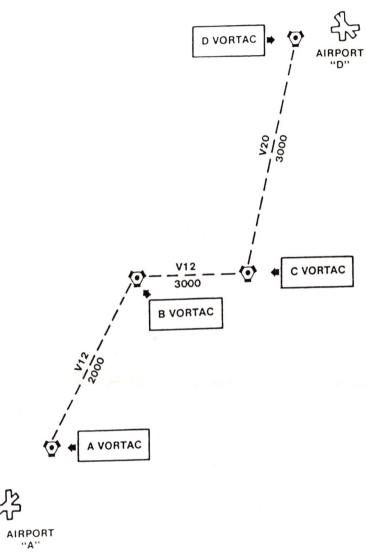

D VORTAC

AIRPORT
"D"

V20
3000

V12
3000

C VORTAC

B VORTAC

V12
2000

A VORTAC

AIRPORT
"A"

Diagram "GG"

Page 157

You:	"Three four Bravo unable Center 120.2."
ATC:	"Cessna three four Bravo try 124.5 if unable, return this frequency."
You:	"Three four Bravo."...you try 124.5 and this time it works.

Occasionally, ATC will have a radio frequency outage which causes ATC's radio to fail. Most Centers have a backup radio that takes about sixty seconds to hook up. So, if you suddenly discover the outage has occured, don't panic. Wait about a minute and try again. If you are still unable to contact ATC, hunt around in your charts for a different frequency close to your location. If you get no response call the flight service station nearest you. The FSS has a direct land line (telephone) to ARTCC (Center) and can relay messages as well as give you a new frequency to try. If that fails follow the FAR lost communications procedure outlined later in this chapter.

Being in radar contact makes IFR flying a lot easier. Unfortunately, radar outages do occur, and when they do it is back to the good old days of manual Center and manual Approach Control. The Center, without radar, must rely on pilot position reports to keep track of all the flights. It is important to be as accurate as possible because your estimates will be used to avoid other IFR aircraft. The format of the position report is quite straight forward.It starts with who you are and where you are and includes the time at the fix. Next, your estimated time of arrival at the next fix, and the name of the next succeding fix along your route of flight. If the weather you are encountering has <u>not</u> been forcast, then include your flight conditions.

For example, your flight routing is A B C D all of which are compulsory reporting points (a solid colored-in triangle on the charts). Refer again to diagram GG. Prior to reaching B you have been informed that radar contact is lost over B vortac you say, "Center, Cessna three four Bravo over B at :20, estimate C at :55, D next, turbulence light to moderate."

ATC: "Cessna three four Bravo thank you."

If you see your time is going to be off more than three minutes you must call ATC with a revision of your time estimates. Now, you arrive over C at :57.

You: "Oakland Center, Cessna three four Bravo over C at :57, estimate D at :15, D airport next." And so on and so on.

When giving time estimates it is easier to just state the minutes past the present hour. However, there is no rule that says you can't give the full time, in Zulu of course.

Position reports must be given even if you have filed "VFR on top."

If a <u>no radar</u> condition exists the following additional reports are manditory <u>without</u> being asked to report them by ATC.

a) When leaving a final <u>approach fix inbound on final approach</u>. Example - "Cessna three four Bravo outer marker inbound."

b) <u>ETA estimates in excess of three minutes from those previously stated.</u> Example - "Cessna three four Bravo, revise my estimate to C to zero one."

Non-radar environment position reports are used extensively outside the United States, so, if you are travelling to Mexico, be ready to give reports automatically.

The following reports must always be made without being requested by ATC, regardless of the radar environment:

a) Time and altitude (or flight level) upon reaching a holding fix or point to which cleared. Example - "Cessna three four Bravo entering holding at C, 9,000 feet at :10."

b) When leaving an assigned holding fix or point. Example - "Cessna three four Bravo leaving holding at C."

c) Change in the average true airspeed (at cruising altitude) when it varies by 5% or 10 knots (whichever is greater) from that filed in the flight plan. Example - "Cessna three four Bravo, Center, change my true airspeed estimate to 135 knots."

d) When vacating any previously assigned altitude or flight level for a newly assigned altitude or flight level. Example - ATC: "Cessna three four Bravo descend and maintain 8,000." You: "Three four Bravo leaving 9,000 to 8,000," or if the controller says, "...pilot's descretion to 8,000," when you are ready to start down say, "Three four Bravo leaving nine for eight."

e) When an altitude change will be made if operating on a clearance that specifies "VFR conditions on top." Example - "Center, three four Bravo, I'm going to climb to 8,500 to avoid weather."

f) When an approach has been missed. Example - "Tower, Cessna three four Bravo missed approach."

Operation in Restricted Airspace

Operating IFR has many advantages over VFR flying. Unlike VFR flying, where permission must be obtained prior to flying in restricted airspace, IFR operators can sometimes fly through restricted airspace without going through the hassle of paperwork or phone calls.

Restricted areas come in two forms, those that are **joint-use** and those that are **nonjoint-use. Joint-use** is a term meaning that both military and civil aircraft can use the restricted airspace. In areas where the military does not continually occupy this airspace, civil aircraft are permitted to transit. Joint-use restricted areas have the name of the controlling agency shown on the En Route chart. Nonjoint-use restricted areas say "No A/G" on the chart.

When flying IFR, Center will know what restricted areas are available to civil aircraft and has the authority to allow aircraft to penetrate the restricted airspace. The pilot does not have to get prior permission. It is important to remember that if you are given a clearance that will ultimately result in your flying into a restricted area, then the restricted area has been released to joint-use. The Center will not issue specific clearance to enter. By virtue of the fact that you are being allowed to fly an airway or heading through restricted airspace, you can rest assured that it is O.K.. If you have gained permission to fly through nonjoint-use airspace you must advise the ATC facility.

Sometimes certain altitudes are reserved for civil aircraft through joint-use airspace when the military is using a portion of the restricted area. The Airman's Information Manual refers to this as an "approved reservation mission".

Holding

A discussion of holding patterns can not be fully understood unless the reasons for holding and the procedures associated with holding are incorporated into the discussion. Beginning instrument students probably fear holding instructions more than any other phase of their training. There are two reasons for this, lack of orientation to surroundings and ATC phraseology. Some students feel they have a clear understanding of what is to be done while doing holding pattern drills with their instructor on the ground, but get disoriented and confused when asked to perform holding patterns in the aircraft. Holding patterns, in most areas of the U.S. are rarely used as a method to delay arrivals. The ATC system and it's computer network have given controllers more time to plan ahead, therefore lessening the need for holding. The holding pattern is used more extensively as a procedure in executing various IFR approaches.

Long after a pilot has acquired an instrument rating, little, if any, actual practice is done to keep current on this particular skill. Orientation and the proper execution of holding instructions should be a constant study throughout a pilot's flying career. Phraseology in holding pattern instructions from ATC are, at first, awesome to the instrument student but simple once fully understood.

When considering holding patterns, it is important to keep things in their proper perspective. First, know your priorities! "Aviate, Navigate, Communicate," has always been the old adage. It means don't drop your pencil, pick it up, and find yourself in a diving spiral. It means talk on the radio but don't forget to turn onto the airway as you intercept it. As you become a more accomplished instrument pilot you will be able to do all these things simultaneously with time left over to call the FSS for an updated weather briefing.

When learning holding patterns in a light instrument trainer, don't clutter your mind with holding pattern speed limits. The maximum limit for propeller driven aircraft is 175 knots indicated airspeed. Few light aircraft can cruise at 175 knots. Most fly much slower. The maximum speed for jets and other high performance aircraft depend on altitude: 0 - 6,000 feet MSL, 200 knots indicated airspeed; 6,000 - 14,000 feet MSL, 210 knots indicated airspeed; 14,000 feet and above, 230 knots indicated airspeed. If you are learning to fly in a propeller driven aircraft, you couldn't get 175 knots out of your aircraft if you used full throttle descending straight down. The Airman's Information Manual says, "When an aircraft is three minutes or less from a clearance limit and a clearance beyond the fix has not been received, the pilot is expected to start a speed reduction so that he will cross the fix at or below the maximum holding airspeed." My point here is that even if you forget about this rule to slow down before entering the holding pattern, you wouldn't be breaking the speed limit in a light aircraft. Instructors often insist on their students slowing down before a holding pattern entry, not because they are too fast now, but to have the student be cognizant of slowing down should the student ever start flying faster aircraft. It is better to stay oriented, fly the airplane and not worry so much about speed limits when first learning holding patterns. A constant airspeed is more important in the execution of a precision holding pattern. The idea of a maximum speed and use of a standard rate turn is to keep you within a designated holding area. Look ahead to diagram II, it illustrates a holding pattern within a designated holding area.

If you have been given a clearance limit other than your destination airport, you will be expecting further clearance prior to reaching your clearance limit fix. If you reach your clearance limit fix and have not received further clearance you are required to enter a holding pattern and request further clearance. *Some confusion has arisen over this because of the problem of lost communications. My best advise is to attempt to get further clearance well before reaching the clearance limit. This will help clear up the question of whether to hold or proceed.* If your clearance contains **EFC (expect further clearance)** or an **EAC (expect approach clearance)** time, it should be written down and not commited to memory. The EFC and EAC are for the sole purpose of a possible communications failure. If the EFC time has lapsed ask for an updated EFC. The same thing goes for an EAC time.

Let's say that your clearance limit is D vortac and you were told to hold at D and to expect further clearance at :30. See diagram HH. Sometime after this clearance was issued, you experienced radio failure. You arrive at D vortac at :26. You must hold at D until :30, then leave the holding fix and proceed to the airport, shoot the approach and land. Don't worry, ATC will have cleared the area for you and is expecting you to follow this rule of lost communications.

If you get the same clearance limit of D vortac but get an expect approach clearance of :30 then the procedure varies. You calculate that from the D vortac to the initial approach fix (in this case the outer compass locator) it will take you four minutes. The lost communications rule with an EAC time is that you are to leave the point to which

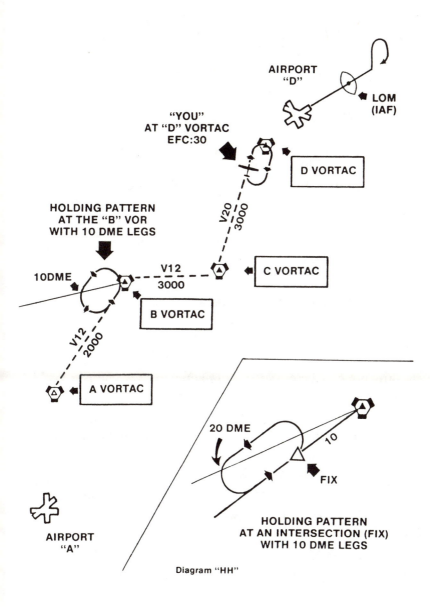

AIRPORT
"D"

LOM
(IAF)

"YOU"
AT "D" VORTAC
EFC:30

D VORTAC

HOLDING PATTERN
AT THE "B" VOR
WITH 10 DME LEGS

V20
3000

10DME

V12
3000

C VORTAC

B VORTAC

V12
2000

A VORTAC

20 DME

10

FIX

HOLDING PATTERN
AT AN INTERSECTION (FIX)
WITH 10 DME LEGS

AIRPORT
"A"

Diagram "HH"

Page 165

cleared so as to arrive over the initial approach fix at the stated time. In our example, no holding would be required because if you reach D at :26 you will be over the IAF (initial approach fix) at :30.

A great many commonly used holding patterns are depicted on your En Route charts. A holding pattern is ATC's way of dealing with rush hour traffic. Aircraft are separated by altitude and stacked up over a fix. Then aircraft are let down in the stack one at a time, until all aircraft are 1,000 feet lower than when they entered the stack. See diagram II. New arrivals to the holding pattern are placed at the top of the stack. It is very important to listen carefully for your call sign and to the call signs of others because a missheard call sign could be disasterous. Imagine if the guy at the bottom of the stack is told to descend to 2,000 feet and the guy at the top thought the descent was for him and started down!

ATC Holding Instructions

From reading your IFR textbook you know that a typical holding pattern resembles a racetrack shape. Holding instructions will be issued in relation to a holding fix. A holding fix means the same as a holding point or holding place. Simply, it is the spot where you place your racetrack pattern. The holding fix will be a point that can be located by use of your navigation radios and is either a VOR, a charted intersection, a DME position along a radial, a non-directional beacon (NDB), or a fan type marker in conjunction with a localizer.

The Airman's Information Manual separates holding instructions into two categories - general holding instructions and detailed holding instructions. Holding instructions are given and modified by ATC on a regular basis.

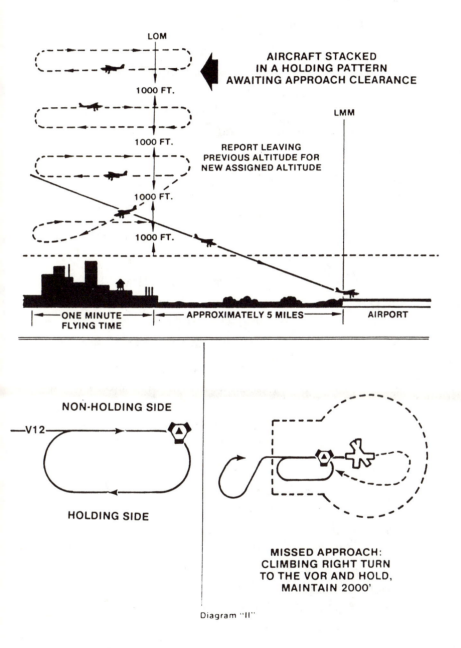

LOM

AIRCRAFT STACKED
IN A HOLDING PATTERN
AWAITING APPROACH CLEARANCE

1000 FT.

LMM

1000 FT.

REPORT LEAVING
PREVIOUS ALTITUDE FOR
NEW ASSIGNED ALTITUDE

1000 FT.

1000 FT.

1000 FT.

ONE MINUTE
FLYING TIME

APPROXIMATELY 5 MILES

AIRPORT

NON-HOLDING SIDE

V12

HOLDING SIDE

MISSED APPROACH:
CLIMBING RIGHT TURN
TO THE VOR AND HOLD,
MAINTAIN 2000'

Diagram "II"

Page 167

The items that could be issued are listed below, followed by an example of their use.

1) The direction to hold from the holding fix.

2) The name of the holding fix.

3) The specified radial, course, magnetic bearing, airway number or jet route.

4) The length in minutes of the inbound leg or if DME or RNAV equipment is used, the length of the outbound leg in nautical miles.

5) The direction of the holding pattern turns.

6) The time to expect further clearance or to expect approach clearance.

Let's suppose that we are between A and B vortacs on V12 heading towards B. Refer back to diagram HH.

ATC:	"Cessna three four Bravo, I have an amendment to your clearance, advise when ready to copy."
You:	"Three four Bravo, go ahead."
ATC:	"Cessna three four Bravo hold southwest of B on Victor 12, left turns, one minute legs, maintain niner thousand, expect further clearance at :20, time now :05."
You:	read back the clearance...

To break the clearance down, ATC said to hold southwest of B. B is our holding fix. Next the approximate location that our racetrack should be placed, is stated in terms of the eight points of the compass. You can see as you look at V12 on diagram HH, it is approximately southwest of B vortac. By virtue of the fact that you were instructed to hold at B on V12 means that the inbound leg of your racetrack should be on the radial V12. Next, ATC

Page 168

said left turns, meaning that your holding pattern should be made up of a series of left turns once established into the racetrack. If ATC did not mention the direction of turns in his clearance, then the pilot should assume right turns are to be flown. Right turns in a holding pattern are considered standard. (Don't confuse this with the traffic pattern where left turns are standard!)

Next, ATC stated one minute legs, this means that the pilot should, once established in a holding pattern, adjust the outbound leg for the wind so that the inbound leg time is one minute to the fix. This statement is a typical ATC add-on because the rules associated with holding patterns already state that if holding at 14,000 feet MSL or below, the inbound leg will be one minute, and above 14,000 feet, one and a half minutes. If ATC desires a different leg time, they will so state.

Usually, high performance aircraft have DME (distance measuring equipment) and RNAV (area navigation). RNAV moves a VOR to where you want it from where it was. Once you are proficient with RNAV use in holding patterns, it will be easy to understand why people buy this equipment. Aircraft that have DME are often given holding instructions that incorporate DME outbound distances rather than timing of the legs.

ATC: "Cessna three four Bravo hold south-
                        west of B, left turns, ten mile legs..."

This means that instead of timing your legs you proceed outbound, in this case to 10 DME and turn inbound. If the fix is not the VOR, but rather an intersection, 10 DME from the station, then with 10 mile legs issued, you would turn inbound when your DME said 20 nautical miles as in the illustration HH.

The next portion of your holding clearance is the altitude at which you are to hold and your expect further clearance time or expect approach clearance time. The altitude that you are issued may be your present altitude, but it may differ, so listen carefully. As you copy this holding clearance, if there is a question in your mind as to the altitude specified, ask ATC, "Verify holding altitude for three four Bravo."

The EFC or EAC may also include a new routing or a new altitude to expect. In the event of a communications failure, you then have the desired altitude and routing that ATC wishes. We will now examine a few additional procedures of lost communication.

Lost Communications

Lost communication procedures are broken down into what I call "What's my ..." categories. If I lose communications with ATC - What's my routing? In short, the answer is the same as your EFC routing. If you didn't get one, then how were you last cleared before the communications failure? Even if you were originally cleared by a routing not requested in your flight plan, you must fly that clearance routing. If you were cleared as filed, then follow your filed flight plan routing.

What's my altitude? Again, you start with the EFC altitude last assigned, original clearance, or filed altitude, whichever was the latest ATC clearance. Remember, it is not uncommon for the last assigned altitude to be below the minimum en route altitude (MEA) on your airway farther down the road. In addition, a minimum crossing altitude (MCA) may be published at the MEA change point. In that case, you must climb before reaching the MEA change point so you'll be at the MCA altitude before you proceed down the airway. When the MEA becomes lower than your last assigned altitude, you are expected to descend to your last assigned altitude again.

What's my time requirement? In the previous holding instructions you were told to expect further clearance at :20 and that the current time was :05. ATC is saying that if we lose communications, we should proceed along our way at 20 minutes past the hour. The reason for giving the current time is a way of synchronizing watches and he is saying that it is five minutes past the present hour. The Airman's Information Manual suggests that as pilots, we be as accurate as possible. If you calculate that you will arrive at the fix a little early, you should slow down to make the time of crossing the fix and proceding on, as close to :20 as you can. One reason I suggest a speed reduction prior to reaching the fix, is that if you arrive at the fix at :19 you would have to enter a holding pattern that will take four minutes to complete, and now you would cross the fix at :23, three minutes late.

Expect approach clearance time means you must leave the holding fix so as to arrive over the initial approach fix at the EAC time stated. If no EAC was issued, then use your time calculated on your actual time of departure plus your filed estimated time en route.

There are a lot of "What if..." questions associated with lost communications, but there is no substitute for common sense in dealing with the problem. For instance, "Land as soon as practical," does not mean you must land as soon as possible. Read the FARs, read your IFR textbook, and know your procedures.

Holding Pattern Airspace

Locations that ATC issues for holding will be areas that have holding pattern airspace. There is an imaginary roped-off area that has been selected for holding. The altitude assigned will give legal terrain clearance as well as legal reception of the navaids involved.

As the illustration II indicates, there is a holding side and a non-holding side of the airway. The holding side is the only side that guarantees terrain clearance and reception of navaids. Actually, there is a little space reserved on the non-holding side for original holding pattern entry using the parallel outbound entry procedure. ATC may be too busy to notice you if you stray from the holding airspace. If ATC notices you are straying from the holding area he may vector you back into place, but the pilot should not rely on this help. It is still the pilot's responsibility to remain oriented and to comply with ATC's instructions.

If you are given a hold and a lengthy wait in the holding pattern, some pilots if issued 10 DME legs, will request 20 DME legs to reduce the number of turns required. If approved, it makes your holding pattern obviously larger. If not approved, it is probably because to do so would take you outside the holding area.

Chapter XIX

IFR Arrival Procedures

The STAR

There are numerous ways for IFR aircraft to arrive at their destination. Some methods are complex and others are rather simple. We will begin this chapter with a discussion of the **Standard Terminal Arrival Route (STAR)**. STAR procedures are often used by ATC to cut down excess verbiage on the radio. A STAR is to arriving what a SID is to departing. A STAR chart depicts in textual, and illustrates in diagram form, a routing and altitude procedure to the destination airport. Every STAR has a name such as the "Modesto Two Arrival." If you are cleared for a STAR, you simply fly the stated procedures in the STAR chart. Occasionally, ATC will want you to fly the STAR routing but not the altitudes depicted. In that case, ATC would say, "Cessna three four Bravo cleared for the Modesto Two Arrival, maintain niner thousand." Or, "Cessna three four Bravo, fly the arrival routing, maintain niner thousand." ATC has then modified the altitudes but wishes you to fly the routing because of traffic separation requirements.

Flow Control

Increasingly, ATC **flow control** is being implemented. It is a way of minimizing the impact of aircraft noise as well as a means of fuel conservation. Flow control starts with possible **gate holds** to cut down on holding time in the air.

A **gate hold** means waiting on the ground instead of holding later in the air. En route speed adjustments for aircraft filed the same direction, are used as a way of spacing aircraft for arrival. Flow control in the approach phase takes the form of a **profile descent**. A **profile descent** is similar to a STAR. Profile descents usually incorporate crossing altitudes that are generally stated as, "cross the fix between 14,000 feet and 17,000 feet..." or "cross between flight level 200 and 17,000 feet." Hard crossing altitudes are generally not incorporated in profile descents, but instead crossing parameters are depicted on the profile descent charts to allow the pilot to adjust his descent according to the descent requirements of his aircraft. Incorporated in the profile descents may be speed adjustments and headings to fly. As always, ATC may delete any or all restrictions on the profile. For example, "Cessna three four Bravo cleared for the low profile, delete the speed."

ATC may also change your speed early, "Cessna three four Bravo slow to 100 knots, cleared for the low profile descent." In this case, you would slow to 100 knots immediately, but descend according to the profile on your chart.

Profile descents are used extensively with high performance aircraft.

Approach Control

As you approach your destination airport, Center will hand you off to Approach Control. Approach Control may or may not have radar.

Radar Approach Control is used not only for ASR (surveillance radar) and PAR (precision approach radar) approaches, but also to provide vectors for an ILS, VOR, NDB, LDA, or TACAN approaches. Radar vectors expedite traffic flow to the airport or to the final approach segment. Often ATC utilizes radar to separate aircraft on approach rather than altitude being a sole means of separation. Let's start with a hypothetical flight where we are with Center, and are subsequently handed off to Approach Control.

ATC: "Cessna three four Bravo, Center, contact Bay Approach now on 133.95."

You: "Three four Bravo, 133.95, good day."

You: "Bay Approach, Cessna three four Bravo descending to eight thousand, passing eight thousand five hundred with information Foxtrot."

ATC: "Cessna three four Bravo radar contact, descend and maintain four thousand, fly present heading, vector for the ILS 26R."

You: "Three four Bravo, present heading, descending to four thousand."

If you don't have a glide slope receiver but have localizer capability, then you must advise ATC.

You: "Three four Bravo request localizer approach."

ATC: "Three four Bravo, roger, present heading for the localizer (approach), runway 26R."

The initial instruction from Approach Control included the instruction to fly the present heading. At this point,

ATC doesn't know exactly what your heading is, only that your track along his radar is in the direction he wants you to go. If he sees you starting to drift off he might say, "Cessna three four Bravo turn ten degrees left, say your new heading."

You: "Three four Bravo left to zero eight zero."

Even if ATC doesn't ask for your new heading, your response should be the same. This keeps ATC informed of your assigned heading.

You now find yourself on an extended left downwind abeam of the outer marker. Shortly you are issued a left base vector heading.

ATC: "Cessna three four Bravo turn left heading 350."

You: "Left 350, three four Bravo."

As you complete your base leg turn, you see that you are about to intercept the localizer but have not been told to do so. Your responsibility as a pilot is to question ATC about his intensions.

You: "Approach, Cessna three four Bravo is this a vector through the localizer?"

ATC: "Three four Bravo I'm sorry, (I forgot to tell you), affirmative, vector through the localizer for spacing behind a heavy DC-10, I'll be turning you back in five miles."

ATC has been known to get distracted. In this case, he might have momentarily forgotten about you and say, "Three four Bravo, turn left heading 260 degrees, three from the marker, cleared for the localizer runway 26 approach, contact the tower over the outer marker, 126.0."

You: "Three four Bravo, 260 degrees, cleared for the approach."

It may not be immediately apparent but this response from ATC has a great deal of pilot information that can be read between the lines. First of all, ATC usually lists approach clearance instructions by beginning with distance from the final approach fix, but in this case ATC issued the intercept heading first, so hopefully, you would begin your turn immediately. The second hint is that of the intercept heading issued. Normally, a vector to the final approach course is within 30 degrees of the final approach heading. The fact that ATC issued an intercept heading that was the same as the inbound heading tells the pilot that he is very close to overshooting final approach. The Airman's Information Manual reminds us that, "A pilot is not expected to turn inbound on the final approach course unless an approach clearance has been issued."

Cancellation of the IFR Flight Plan

The remainder of this chapter deals with the various types of approach procedures utilized to complete an IFR flight. Although these procedures differ, they all conclude with an eventual landing and the cancellation of the IFR flight plan. It is easier to discuss cancellation here and understand that one of these cancellation methods can be used for any of the remaining approaches that will be subsequently discussed.

Radar service is automatically terminated when the landing is complete or the tower controller has the aircraft in sight, whichever occurs first. The latter is referred to as **landing assured.** After landing is assured, at an airport with an operating control tower, the tower automatically cancels your IFR flight plan. Your cancellation will release the next aircraft for an IFR approach or an IFR departure in cases where a missed approach procedure specifies a return to the initial approach fix for holding (as shown in diagram II). When the missed approach specifies a straight out procedure that will not conflict with IFR inbounds, several IFR aircraft may be inbound with distance separation provided by ATC.

I would like to touch upon the situation where an aircraft is awaiting IFR release which is dependant upon you completing your IFR approach to a landing.

In the course of your instrument instruction, you will probably notice that your instructor sometimes gives you his own clearance for practice and you legally depart or arrive VFR. He watches for traffic and you fly "under the hood." This is an excellent way to save time and money. However, there comes a time in your training when you have to start "filing" and going under IFR rules. Even if it's a nice day, your instructor will have you file an IFR flight plan. This is so you get used to working the system from the original clearance, to the final hand-off to the tower. You won't be the only aircraft wishing to enter the IFR system. Other aircraft, practicing or not, will be waiting to use the IFR system. Let's say that it is a beautiful VFR day around the field that you are making an IFR approach to. You approach the VOR, which in this case is the final approach fix, and are handed off to the tower. There are several IFR aircraft waiting for Departure Control release sitting on the ground burning up money. The tower can't release any of these aircraft because legally if you make a missed approach, you must return to the VOR and hold. This is depicted in diagram JJ. If you proceed with the

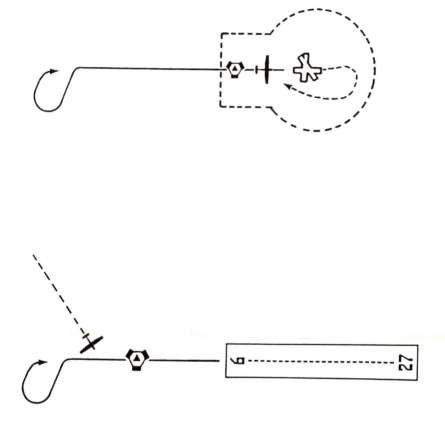

Diagram "JJ"

Page 179

missed approach, it is legally impossible for the tower to release an aircraft IFR unless you land or landing is assured. Approach Control can not clear another IFR aircraft for an approach to that airport either, until your landing is assured. So what can you do to help everybody else out and still get your practice in? One suggestion is this, when you are handed off to the tower say, "Tower, Cessna three four Bravo VOR inbound, landing assured, cancel IFR, request to continue approach VFR, full stop."

ATC:	"Three four Bravo roger, continue to runway niner, number two following a Cherokee on left base, break, Gulfstream zero zero Papa cleared for take-off."
You:	"Three four Bravo."
300P:	"Cleared for take-off, Gulfstream zero zero Papa."
ATC:	"Zero zero Papa contact departure, good day."
300P:	"Zero Zero Papa, good day."

Your first contact with the tower was reporting your position as required, which was the final approach fix inbound (assuming there is no radar in the tower). The next portion of your call was that you canceled your IFR flight plan earlier than the tower could legally have done. *ATC must wait until he has you in sight and has determined that landing is assured.* Next, you included that you would still like to continue the approach but under VFR rules of see and avoid, rather than immediately breaking off the approach and entering the traffic pattern. ATC approved, and issued traffic to follow as if you were making a straight-in entry VFR. In addition, ATC was able to release the Gulfstream into the IFR system prior to your arrival because you released the airspace by cancelling your flight plan. I hope that while you are working on your IFR rating or just keeping proficient, that you follow this advice whenever you can.

Cancellation of an IFR flight plan is not automatic at airports without a control tower. If only a FSS exists, after landing you must say, "Red Bluff radio, Cessna three four Bravo clear of the active (runway), cancel IFR." You can also use the previous suggestion of cancelling in the air when landing is assured. Remember, the weather must be VFR. You can't use this method to expedite other IFR traffic if the field is below VFR minimums.

When approaching an uncontrolled field served only by a Unicom or Multicom frequency, Approach Control will say something like "Cessna three four Bravo, three from the VOR, turn left heading 120, cleared straight-in VOR runway 9 approach, maintain two thousand until intercepting final, report cancellation to this facility when on the ground by calling 555-1234 or through Red Bluff radio, change to advisory frequency approved, good day." Quite a mouthful right? Not if you are expecting such a clearance. The clearance starts out with the usual distance from the final approach fix and the fact that it is a straight-in approach, (no procedure turns are required because of use of radar vectors in lieu of the procedure turn). The next information is that you will be landing on runway 9, (to the best of ATC's knowledge the wind is favoring runway 9) as opposed to a VOR approach to runway 9 and then "circle to land runway 27." You are then given instructions on how to cancel your IFR flight plan after you land, followed by the words, "change to advisory frequency approved."

The method of cancellation when on the ground is easy. If they give you a phone number to call Approach Control you can use that. If you walk inside an FBO and find a land line to the local FSS, you can call the FSS and they can relay your cancellation. I have been able to receive Approach Control on the ground after landing at some uncontrolled airports because of good terrain conditions. This is the quickest method of cancellation if you are able. When ATC receives cancellation notice they release the airspace to another IFR user.

The phrase "change to advisory frequency approved" is used instead of saying "contact the tower" because there is no tower. It means radar services are terminated and, in this case, you either tune in Unicom or Multicom, which-ever applies, and broadcast in the blind such information as the type of approach you are executing, your position, and when you are over the final approach fix inbound. Listen and coordinate with other possible traffic at that field. Remember, at many uncontrolled fields there may be aircraft shooting touch and goes at an altitude below controlled airspace — legally flying with one mile visibility and clear of the clouds.

Approach Clearance

The approach clearance will take on many forms de-pending on where you are, what kind of approach facility is available (radar or manual), and what kind of approach you are going to execute.

Let's say that your position is as shown in the diagram KK. You are inbound on V20 to Lodi vortac at 5,000 feet and as you approach Lodi vortac ATC says, "Cessna three four Bravo, cleared ILS runway niner approach, contact the tower over the outer marker on final."

You: "Three four Bravo cleared for the
                         approach."

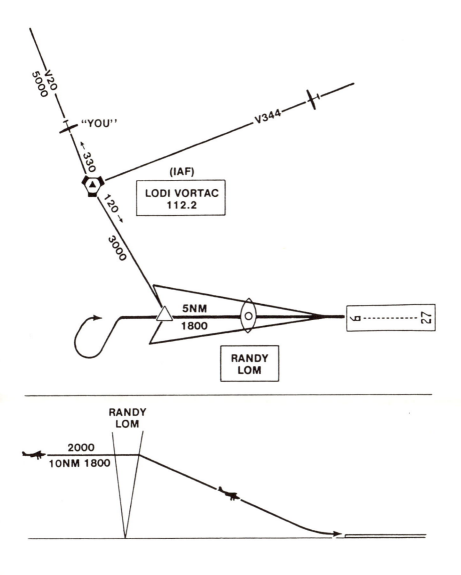

Diagram "KK"

Page 183

Since Lodi vortac is depicted as being an initial approach fix (IAF), you can shoot the approach without having to execute the procedure turn.

You must maintain 5,000 feet while on V20 because that is the MEA. After passing the Lodi vortac and established on the 120 degree radial, the MEA changes to 3,000 feet and you may descend to 3,000 feet. Once you are established on the localizer, you may descend to 1,800 feet until intercepting the glide slope. Once intercepting the glide slope and when passing the outer compass location, you contact the tower and say, "Cessna three four Bravo outer marker inbound." You are subsequently cleared to land or given a landing sequence.

Suppose that you were the aircraft on V344 inbound to Lodi vortac and given an approach clearance. You would have the same routing as the aircraft in the previous example. In the case of our aircraft on V344 there are other options. If you tune in Randy LOM (outer compass locator) and get a good signal, you could request to go direct to the Randy LOM. If you are cleared direct to the Randy LOM you must now execute the depicted procedure turn (still referring to diagram KK). Along with the clearance for "direct Randy," you must be given an altitude to maintain until reaching Randy, because a safe altitude is not charted. If ATC does not give you an altitude then ask for one. Your conversation would go something like this...

You: "Approach, Cessna three four Bravo has Randy suitable, request direct."

ATC: "Cessna three four Bravo cleared direct Randy, maintain four thousand until reaching Randy, cleared ILS runway 9, contact the tower over the outer marker on final."

You:	"Three four Bravo." (Obviously you may read back all or some of that clearance, especially if you're not sure of what was said.)

You as the pilot had determined that it would take less time to go direct to the Randy compass locator and do a procedure turn than it would to proceed to the Lodi vortac and go straight-in via the IAF procedure. After executing the procedure turn and passing the LOM inbound, you contact the tower.

You:	"Tower, Cessna three four Bravo outer marker inbound," or "Randy inbound."
ATC:	"Cessna three four Bravo cleared to land, wind 090 at 20."

When receiving a clearance like "direct Randy," you are listening for the words "direct," "proceed direct," "cleared direct," or "cleared present position direct." All have the same meaning. As the Airman's Information Manual says, "If a pilot is uncertain of his clearance, he should immediately query ATC as to what route of flight is desired."

Depending on the type of IFR charts you are using, a format is used to give you the minimum safe altitude that can be flown in a particular quadrant. If issued an altitude, for example, to fly direct Randy LOM that is lower than the minimum sector altitude, the pilot should verify the altitude again.

ATC:	"Cessna three four Bravo cleared direct Randy, maintain 4,000 until Randy, cleared ILS runway 9..."
You:	"Three four Bravo, roger, I'm showing MSA of 4,500 feet."

| ATC: | "Three four Bravo, roger, my minimum vectoring altitude is 4,000 feet in your area." |
| You: | "Three four Bravo, thank you." |

This is heads up flying (using your head). ATC can make mistakes and he won't be surprised at your question. In many cases, minimum vectoring altitudes (MVA) provide at least a 300 foot clearance above the floor of controlled airspace and keep you at least three miles away from any isolated, prominent obstruction. Use of a MVA by ATC facilitates vectoring around such an obstruction. While being vectored to final, or being allowed to cut the corner on your routing, ATC may utilize a MVA. A MVA also provides for flight 1,000 feet above obstacles in non-mountainous terrain and 2,000 feet above obstacles in designated mountainous terrain.

As previously mentioned, if you are handed off to an approach control facility that does not have radar, it is referred to as a manual approach control facility. You are kept track of on paper rather than radar. Time estimates are needed as well as position reports. When handed off to such a facility, you might be asked for your estimate to Randy. You also might be asked to report "procedure turn outbound" or "procedure turn inbound."

At your airport, there may be several approach procedures available. If there is more than one approach available, ATC may issue "advanced information on the instrument approach." Some of this information can usually be found on the ATIS, but airport conditions might have changed since you last listened to it.

| ATC: | "Cessna three four Bravo fly present heading vector for the ILS runway 9 approach." |

This is the advanced information, an ILS to runway 9. If you don't have ILS capability in your aircraft you must advise ATC immediately.

You: "Three four Bravo unable ILS, request VOR approach to 9."

In this situation, it may be necessary for ATC to withhold your clearance for the VOR approach (a different approach than everybody else is using), until such time as traffic conditions permit. Of course if a pilot is involved in an emergency situation he will be given priority.

At times, ATC will not specify a particular approach procedure in the clearance, but will state, "cleared for the approach". The AIM states that "such a clearance indicates that the pilot may execute any one of the authorized instrument approach procedures for that airport. This clearance does not constitute approval for the pilot to execute a <u>contact</u> approach or a <u>visual</u> approach."

When cleared for an approach, pilots are expected to execute the entire procedure as described on the instrument approach procedure chart unless an appropriate new or revised ATC clearance is received or if the pilot cancels his IFR flight plan by saying, "Cancel IFR."

We have been talking all along about the U.S. Government navaids and approaches. However, it is possible that a privately owned airport might have privately owned navaids. If you are planning to make an IFR approach to that airport, then you must obtain permission from the owner before using it. If you don't, he may turn off the navaid while you are using it for maintenance or energy conservation. The AIM goes on to say that, "approval by the owner is necessary because special procedures are for the exclusive use of the single interest unless otherwise authorized by owner. Air traffic controllers are not required to question pilots to determine if they have permission to use the procedure. Controllers presume a pilot has obtained approval and is aware of any details of the procedure if he files an IFR flight plan to that airport."

Procedure Turns

A **procedure turn** is specified when it is necessary to reverse direction to establish the aircraft inbound on an intermediate or final approach course. The approach chart indicates the length of the procedure turn in terms of distance. Rate of turn and proper time to turn are left up to the pilot. Maximum speed in the procedure turn is 250 knots, although this is a normal speed limit below 10,000 feet anyway.

A holding pattern is sometimes charted in lieu of a procedure turn. If a holding pattern is used, one minute legs or the published length must be observed.

If cleared for the approach prior to returning to the holding fix and the aircraft is at the prescribed altitude, additional circuits of holding are not necessary nor expected by ATC. If a pilot elects to make additional circuits to lose excessive altitude, or to become better established on course, it is the responsibility of the pilot to so advise ATC when the approach clearance is received.

ATC: "Cessna three four Bravo cleared NDB runway 9 approach, contact the tower over the outer marker."

You: "Three four Bravo cleared for the approach, I'll need another couple of turns in holding to lose altitude."

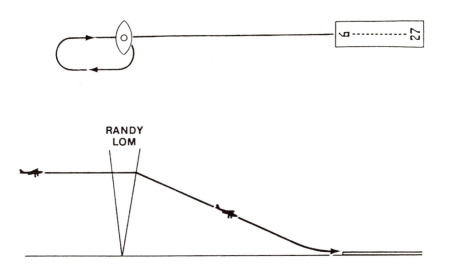

RANDY
LOM

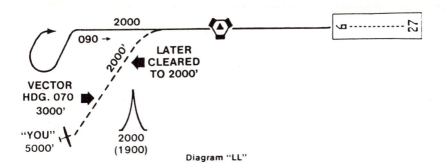

2000

090 →

2000'

LATER
CLEARED
TO 2000'

VECTOR
HDG. 070
3000'

"YOU"
5000'

2000
(1900)

Diagram "LL"

| ATC: | "Three four Bravo, roger, report procedure turn inbound." |
| You: | "Three four Bravo." |

See diagram LL, here is a case where you are in a holding pattern at Randy LOM at 5,000 feet. You have been cleared for the approach but have to lose 3,000 feet before establishing yourself on final at the specified altitude of 2,000 feet. You realize immediately that you can't lose 3,000 feet in one single turn in holding without popping your passengers ear drums, so you have to simply advise ATC that you'll need a couple more racetrack patterns to descend to the proper altitude before commencing the approach. Approach Control approved and asked you to let him know when you would be ready to start inbound to the airport. Upon completion of your descending holding pattern (called a shuttle descent - a climbing hold pattern is called a shuttle climb), as you turn inbound, you advise ATC.

You:	"Cessna three four Bravo procedure turn inbound."
ATC:	"Three four Bravo, roger, contact the tower."
You:	"Three four Bravo."

Sometimes ATC needs a little more warning that you are in a position to make the approach by requesting that you report your procedure turn outbound. So when you are on your last holding pattern before the approach, as you turn outbound, you say, "Cessna three four Bravo procedure turn outbound."

If NOPT is shown on the chart, no pilot may make a procedure turn unless he has requested it and ATC so clears him. A procedure turn is not required when an approach can be made directly from a specified intermediate fix to the final approach fix. In such cases, the term NOPT is charted with the appropriate course and altitude to denote that the procedure turn is not required. If a procedure turn is depicted, or when cleared to do so by ATC, descent below the procedure turn altitude should not be made until the aircraft is established on the inbound course, since some NOPT altitudes may be lower than the procedure turn altitudes.

When a teardrop procedure turn is depicted and a course reversal is needed, this type of turn must be executed.

When a one minute holding pattern replaces the procedure turn, the standard entry and holding pattern shall be followed except if radar vectoring is provided.

Individual approach charts may have additional restrictions not commonly found on most charts, so study the approach chart thoroughly before executing the approach.

Radar Vectoring

Radar vectoring is usually the easiest way to shoot an IFR approach. Radar vectoring requires just as much pilot skill as shooting a full approach under your own navigation.

The most difficult part of flying radar vectors is staying oriented. By this I mean knowing your position from the airport, how much time will be required to descend to the final approach altitude, and when to complete checklists.

Often ATC will issue descent altitudes stated as "pilot's discretion" meaning that you can descend when you want. As he vectors you closer to the final approach, you must know where you are so you don't end up too high when he turns you on final approach. If he sees you are still kind of high he may say, "Cessna three four Bravo are you going to make it down okay if I turn you on final in three miles outside the outer marker?"

You:	"Negative, I'll need a little longer downwind to make it." Or "Affirmative."

Remember it is awfully embarrassing to be given pilot's discretion altitude assignments all the way through the descent only to have to be vectored around a bit more to lose altitude. Keep oriented, know your aircraft and pilot capabilities.

Being vectored for a straight-in approach is pretty simple. The important thing is to listen to your final altitude instructions.

Let's say you are on a wide base leg vector to final as in diagram LL. You are level at your last assigned altitude of 5,000 feet.

ATC:	"Cessna three four Bravo, 10 miles from the outer marker turn left heading 070, cleared straight-in VOR runway 9 approach, maintain 3,000 until established on final."
You:	"Three four Bravo roger, cleared for the approach, 3,000 until on final, leaving 5,000 for 3,000."

Here you are cleared for the approach but can't descend below 3,000 feet until you are on final because of obstacles or terrain even though this approach plate shows 2,000 feet as the altitude to be at upon reaching the final approach fix inbound. If you are approaching the final approach fix and feel that you'll be too high if not permitted to descend to 2,000 feet then advise ATC.

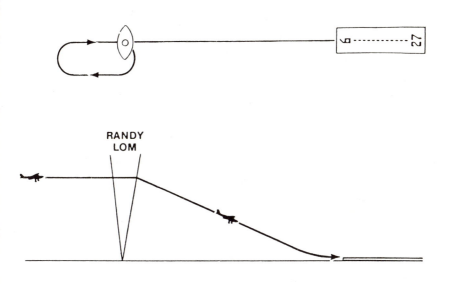

RANDY
LOM

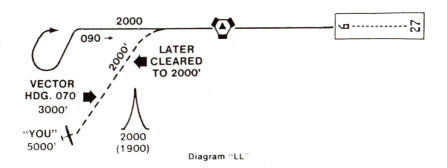

VECTOR
HDG. 070°
3000'

090 →

2000

2000'

LATER
CLEARED
TO 2000'

"YOU"
5000'

2000
(1900)

Diagram "LL"

Page 193

You:	"Cessna three **four Bravo request** lower."
ATC:	"Three four Bravo now maintain 2,000 until intercepting final."

You are now clear of the obstacle that restricted you to 3,000 feet and subsequently cleared to 2,000 feet.

Timed Approaches From a Holding Fix

The technique required to fly a timed approach from a holding fix is outlined in the Airman's Information Manual as well as in other publications. To highlight the communication aspect of this procedure, I will say that the controller might not specifically state the fact that "timed approaches are in progress," but it is understood by virtue of the fact that you have been assigned a time to depart the final approach fix inbound. This procedure is used when ATC has a total radar failure.

Radar Approaches

There are three types of radar approaches, **precision approaches, surveillance,** and **no-gyro approaches.** All that is needed to utilize the service is an operational radio transmitter and receiver. All three types are rarely used by general aviation except as practice during IFR flight training. This training serves as an introduction to the procedures and demonstrates that in a real emergency, like the loss of all navigation radios, or a gyro compass failure, an aircraft can still shoot an approach and land.

Precision approach radar is similar to an ILS except you are talked down by a controller to the runway or decision height.

Precision approach radar (PAR) is refered to as a **ground controlled approach (GCA).** After initial contact you are instructed not to reply to any further transmissions. (This will be a one way conversation from here on out.) You will also be instructed that if you don't hear a transmission for say five seconds or so, you are to make a missed approach and the missed approach instructions are given. The **decision height** will only be given if requested by the pilot.

The PAR procedure begins after the pilot has been vectored to the straight-in final approach course. This vectoring is no different from the normal vectoring to an ILS. After being vectored on to final, the pilot is handed off to the **final controller.** The **final controller** communicates PAR instructions to the pilot. The pilot will be given a 10 to 30 second warning when approaching the glide path. Then the pilot will be instructed to begin descent. You should use the same airspeed and rate of descent as you would doing a normal ILS approach. Adjustments to your heading will be issued in small increments of perhaps two or three degrees, the technique utilized when flying an ILS. Your glide path will be adjusted by using the terms "slightly" or "well above" or "well below" the glide slope. When so instructed, the pilot is expected to correct his glide path as well as heading immediately. If you get too far out of the ballpark, ATC will instruct you to execute a missed approach. Along with this information relating to glide path and azimuth, you are issued distance from the runway at least every mile. Once you cross the runway threshold ATC advisories are in the form of deviation from the runway centerline.

Surveillance radar is usually used for approach coordination (spacing) and vectoring to the final approach course. In a pinch, radar of this type can also be used to conduct an approach. What a PAR is to an ILS, a surveillance approach is to a non-precision approach. The surveillance radar approach is a non-precision approach because no glide slope information is issued by ATC. Azimuth guidance (headings) are issued every mile to the runway. The only altitude instructions given would be step down type altitude assignments and the instructions to descend to the minimum descent altitude.

The pilot will be advised of the position of the missed approach point as well as his position each mile on final. The pilot may request that he be issued recommended altitudes as he progresses on final. These recommended altitudes will be based on the descent gradient established for that airport. If a circle to land maneuver must be accomplished, the pilot informs ATC of the category of aircraft he is flying and ATC issues the appropriate circling minimums. In this case, category of aircraft refers to the A, B, C, or D criteria used to determine decision height and minimum descent altitudes on IFR approach plates.

No-gyro approaches are utilized to aid the pilot in a situation where power to the gyro instruments has been lost. Some IFR student practice in dealing with this situation comes in the form of timing turns. The use of **timed turns** begins with the knowledge that a standard rate turn is defined as a turn that produces a rate of 3 degrees per second heading change. Commonly, pilots use their rate of turn indicator to determine the rate of bank necessary to produce a standard rate turn. A 360 degree heading change will take 2 minutes to accomplish using this standard rate. A 180 degree turn will take one minute, a 90 degree turn 30 seconds. Additionally, your training will include the utilization of the magnetic compass, a skill usually requiring much practice. Both timed turns and magnetic compass are helpful, but extremly difficult when executing IFR approaches. In recognition of this fact, the F.A.A. has established the no-gyro approach procedure. If you lose your gyros inform ATC.

You: "Approach, Cessna three four Bravo, I just lost my gyros, request no-gyro vectors for the approach."

Subsequently, ATC radar vectors will be issued.

ATC: "Three four Bravo turn left."
"Three four Bravo stop turn."
"Three four Bravo turn left."
"Three four Bravo stop turn, 3 from the outer marker, cleared ILS runway 36 R, contact the tower over the outer marker."

ATC is watching your blip on his scope to determine the required heading rather than issue compass headings. The procedure is not as accurate as issuing headings because the controller has to wait for another radar update (another sweep of the radar antenna) to check your progress. You are expected to make all instructed turns at the standard rate. After the pilot is turned onto final approach, all turns should be made at half standard rate. Partial panel flight technique is tough enough as it is with respect to basic aircraft control and therefore use of this no-gyro procedure reduces pilot workload tremendously.

Radar Monitoring of Instrument Approaches

At some joint-use (civil and military) airports a PAR and ILS are available for the same runway. At these particular airports if the weather is below VFR minimums (1000 feet and 3 miles), it is at night, or the pilot has requested such a service, simultaneous PAR advisories will be issued while you are flying the ILS.

The ILS is the primary aid for the approach and the PAR radar is secondary. Prior to starting final approach, the pilot will be given the frequency that he can monitor during his ILS approach. If for any reason radar services cannot be furnished, the pilot will be so advised.

The PAR advisory information will include three important items:

1) The PAR final controller will inform you when you are over the final approach fix inbound. Chances are your marker beacon equipment will be functioning normally, but this advisory serves as a cross check. Remember that an ILS approach can not legally be performed unless the pilot has a means to identify the final approach fix to confirm glide path quality. ILS ground equipment can occasionally send out false signals. These false glide slopes are located above the normal glide slope signal, but will appear to the pilot and his equipment to be a normal glide slope. The only way of checking that you are on the real glide slope on the approach is to check the published altitude on your approach chart. The chart profile view will state the altitude you should be at upon crossing the outer marker (final approach fix) inbound on the real glide

slope. This cross-check of your altitude compared to the published altitude over the final approach fix is referred to as **confirming glide path quality.** Even though our discussion here is concerned with shooting an ILS with a PAR backup, it is important to know that any radar facility can "call the outer marker" for you if your marker beacon equipment has failed.

You:	"Approach, three four Bravo advise me when over the outer marker."
ATC:	"Three four Bravo wilco (will co-operate)."
ATC:	"Three four Bravo, over outer marker now, contact tower."
You:	"Three four Bravo."

ATC confirmation of your position over the final approach fix is a legal substitute for pilot airborne confirmation.

2) The PAR final controller will issue advisories related to pilot deviations from the perfect ILS profile that is portrayed on the ATC scope. If the pilot is executing a non-precision approach (localizer only), then glide path information will not be issued. The descent portion of a non-precision approach does not coincide with the depicted PAR glide path.

3) The PAR final controller will advise the pilot to execute a missed approach if flight proceeds outside the PAR limits. The pilot must then comply with the missed approach command unless he advises ATC that he has the prescribed visual reference for the runway.

You:	"Three four Bravo, runway in sight."

Simultaneous ILS Approaches

Someday, while flying into a busy multiple runway airport, you may hear on the ATIS or directly from Approach Control that "Simultaneous ILS approaches are in progress runways 36L and 36R." This procedure can be legally authorized if the runways involved are at lease 4,300 feet apart. The term **simultaneous ILS approach** means that ATC can allow two aircraft to fly ILSs side by side, each to a different runway.

The moment ATC advises you that simultaneous ILS approaches are in progress, you should notify ATC of any malfunctioning or inoperative receivers. If for some reason you do not wish to participate in this procedure, you should so advise ATC.

Here is how the procedure works. Picture in your mind runways 36L and 36R. Each runway has it's own ILS. ATC vectors you to 36R and another aircraft to 36L. You are both inbound on your respective ILSs side by side. A special **monitor controller** sits at a radar scope and his sole job is to make sure you two do not drift together and collide. If the controller sees an aircraft drifting he will instruct the off-course pilot to get back on his own localizer. These corrective vectors are issued when the aircraft get within 2,000 feet of each other. Let's say the pilot on the left is the one who is drifting towards you. If the controller can't get him to respond to the corrective headings in time, then you will be instructed to alter your course. This is important to know because if you are flying your usual perfect ILS and are suddenly told to alter course you will understand that the instructions were not issued because you were at fault.

The Airman's Information Manual states that whenever simultaneous ILS approaches are in progress, radar advisories will be provided on the tower frequency. The controller that is monitoring your progress down the ILS has the capability to override the tower controller if corrective action is necessary to separate you and the pilot on the left. The monitoring of your approaches will automatically terminate one mile from the runway, or if procedurally required, at a specific location like the ILS middle marker. The monitor controller will not advise the pilot when the monitoring has been terminated.

The next subject deals with a similar, but slightly different procedure called the **parallel approach.**

Parallel Approaches

Parallel approaches are an ATC procedure that permits ILS approaches to parallel runways having a centerline distance of at least 2,500 feet apart. A parallel approach differs from a simultaneous approach not only in the runway centerline distance, but also in that there is no radar monitoring and advisory requirement. A staggered separation of aircraft on the adjacent localizer is required for parallel approaches.

The staggering of aircraft is done as follows:

1) A minimum of 2 miles separation is required between successive aircraft on the adjacent localizer course.

2) A minimum of 3 miles between aircraft on the same localizer.

3) During turns on to the localizer, vertical separation of 1,000 feet and 3 miles between the aircraft is used.

If the tower does not have radar, the approach controller has the capability to override the tower frequency if a sudden need for additional separation is needed.

At airports where simultaneous ILS approaches are used and a pilot requests that he <u>not</u> be given a simultaneous approach, then ATC will adjust the aircraft's speed until a legal staggering is accomplished, thereby making his approach a parallel approach.

Side-Step Maneuver

The side-step maneuver is usually used when there is only one ILS to an airport with parallel runways. If the runways are 1,200 feet apart or less, this maneuver can be legally authorized.

This procedure is a way of using one ILS to the best advantage. The landing minimums are higher than for a straight-in ILS, but usually lower than circling minimums. When the weather permits, ATC may say, "Cessna three four Bravo cleared ILS runway 36L, side-step 36R." The pilot is expected to transition to the right runway as soon as practical after having the runway environment in sight.

Missed Approach

If you have missed the approach you must advise ATC. You must fly the published missed approach procedure unless it has been revised by ATC. If ATC issues you a turn other than what is specified by the missed approach procedure on your approach plate, then other factors that you are not aware of exist and you should follow the new instructions. Perhaps an aircraft has just taken off before your arrival and if you execute the missed approach procedure as published, there might be a conflict.

An important point about executing a missed approach procedure is to include in your advisory to ATC your next intentions. For example:

You: "Tower, three four Bravo, missed approach, request vectors back for another ILS approach." Or, "Cessna three four Bravo missed approach, would like to proceed to my alternate - Oakland."

This way the tower can better coordinate with Approach Control when they know what you specifically want.

Contact and Visual Approaches

Although most instrument approaches utilize navigation radios in conjunction with associated navaids, there are two types of approaches that do not. It is important to understand their differences as well as their individual limitations in order to incorporate them into your instrument skills.

The **contact approach** is an IFR approach and must specifically be requested by the pilot. The pilot may request a **contact approach** if the reported ground visibility is at least 1 mile. A contact approach can only be approved by ATC for airports that already have an instrument approach procedure prescribed for that airport. In other words, if there isn't an approach plate published for that airport, then you can not make a contact approach there. The AIM reminds us that, ATC may not solicit a contact approach from the pilot." If the pilot requests a contact approach he can reasonably expect to continue to the airport of destination with 1 mile visibility remaining clear of the clouds. In addition, the pilot must maintain his own terrain clearance. A contact approach enables the pilot to deviate from the prescribed instrument approach procedure and to navigate on his own to the airport.

If ATC clears you for the contact approach, he may issue you missed approach instructions. If you do not receive specific missed approach instructions then you would follow the published missed approach instructions stated on the approach chart to that airport.

By now, I'm sure that you can see that a contact approach is similar to the Special VFR procedure. The big difference is that a contact approach is an IFR approach and has priority over Special VFR operations. Contact approaches are commonly used by the pilot to eliminate the need of executing the prescribed instrument approach procedure. It saves time. The AIM sums it up very well. "A contact approach is an approach procedure that may be used by a pilot (with prior authorization from ATC) in lieu of conducting a standard or special instrument approach procedure to an airport. It is not intended for use by a pilot on an IFR flight clearance to operate to an airport not having an authorized instrument approach procedure. Nor is it intended for an aircraft to conduct an IFR approach to one airport and when "in the clear" to discontinue that approach and proceed to another airport."

A situation where you might elect to perform a contact approach rather than other prescribed approaches would be while being vectored towards the airport. As you are being vectored, you sight the airport, or landmarks associated with the airport. Rather than traveling additional miles to be vectored for the approach, you decide a contact approach would be more expenditious.

You:	"Approach, Cessna three four Bravo request contact approach."
ATC:	"Cessna three four Bravo cleared for the contact approach, contact the tower 119.7."
You:	"Three four Bravo."

When the pilot is handed off to the tower radar service is automatically terminated. Upon establishing contact with the tower, you would be sequenced into the traffic pattern and land. *I feel compelled to caution you about contact approaches. Professional airmen assess the circumstances carefully when contemplating a contact approach and so should you. Safety should never be compromised to save time.*

The **visual approach** is probably the most widely issued IFR authorization. A visual approach can be solicited by ATC or requested by the pilot. ATC authorization for a visual approach does not alter IFR flight plan cancellation requirements. IFR separation parameters were established for safety but also to deal with radar limitations. Aircraft that may appear close on radar may be adequately separated visually from the cockpit. For this reason, the visual approach concept was incorporated into the IFR system.

The procedures are quite straight forward. Approach Control may be vectoring you for the ILS fully aware that the present weather is VFR. Because of the ATC altitude restrictions in the course of these vectors, you elect to request a visual approach.

You:	"Approach, Cessna three four Bravo has the airport insight." Or, "have airport, request visual."

| ATC: | "Three four Bravo cleared visual approach runway 26." |
| You: | "Three four Bravo cleared for the visual 26." |

Even though ATC is aware of the VFR conditions in existance, he still must play the game as if it is a stormy IFR night, until a visual approach is issued. In addition, even though you have been cleared for the visual, you must still remain on Approach Control's frequency until handed off to the tower.

Acceptance of the visual approach by the pilot relinquishes ATC from terrain avoidance. If you are issued a visual clearance that specifies following another aircraft, then you are also now responsible for wake turbulence avoidance. If you have the airport in sight, but not the aircraft you are to follow, then ATC assumes the responsibility for traffic separation and wake turbulence. All you have to do is get your flying machine to the runway and land.

It is important to know that a visual approach is not an instrument approach, therefore, there is technically no missed approach procedure. A missed approach from a visual approach takes the form of a **VFR go-around.** Visual approaches can be issued to one aircraft on one runway while other VFR or IFR aircraft are conducting approaches to another runway. The F.A.A. criteria for this operation is quite simple. If the parallel runways are separated by less than 2,500 feet, then all aircraft must have each other in sight. If the distance is greater, then the pilots operating on respective runways need only be advised that operations are taking place on the other runway. *One note for IFR pilots operating in the TCA, if you are cleared for a visual approach you are not authorized to operated beneath the floor of the TCA.*

You do not have to accept a visual approach if you don't want it.

ATC:	"Cessna three four Bravo fly heading 260, the airport is at 12 o'clock and 5 miles."
You:	"Three four Bravo, it's a little hazy, we'd like the approach today."
ATC:	"Roger three four Bravo, fly heading 230, maintain 3,000, vector to the 26 localizer."
You:	"Three four Bravo."

Landing Priority

When you are cleared for an IFR approach, the clearance does not imply that you have landing priority over other aircraft. Towers handle aircraft on a first come, first serve basis regardless of the type of flight plan when the weather is VFR.

Landing sequence will be issued by the tower as soon as possible. When handed off to the tower, the conversation might go like this:

You:	"Tower, Cessna three four Bravo, ILS inbound."
Tower:	"Three four Bravo, roger, continue, not in sight."
You:	"Three four Bravo."
You:	"Three four Bravo, outer marker inbound."
Tower:	"Three four Bravo in sight, number two following a Bonanza on right base."
You:	"Three four Bravo, in sight, (I have the traffic), number two."

Page 207

Pop-up Clearances

A **pop-up clearance** is where you just pop-up un-announced, call ATC and get an IFR clearance without previously filing an IFR flight plan. During the time this book was written, **pop-up clearances** (air filed) were being turned down by ATC due to controller workload restrictions brought on by the PATCO strike. As the system stabilizes and returns to normal, air filing will be restored also.

I have always recommended to my students to file IFR whenever possible for practice or whenever the weather is marginal. However, the use of your IFR "ticket" is not limited to cross country flight from point A to point B. It is probably most widely used to go from IFR to VFR on top, and from VFR over the top to an IFR approach and landing.

Let's say that you are flying home VFR and discover that your destination airport has gone below basic VFR mini-mums (1,000 foot ceiling, 3 miles visibility). You get your IFR approach plate out and tune in the ATIS, confirm the weather, and find that the VOR to runway 19R is in use. You then brief yourself for the approach and position yourself so as to be easily identified by radar and in an area where an approach clearance can be readily issued such as a VOR or intersection which is a segment of the initial approach. Now you are ready to call ATC and get an IFR clearance to your destination airport. We start with the initial call up in case ATC is busy.

You:	"Approach, Cessna one two three four Bravo."
ATC:	"Cessna three four Bravo, Travis Approach."

You:	"Three four Bravo holding over the Concord VOR, VFR at 3,500 feet, request IFR approach to Concord. I'm a Cessna 182 slant Uniform."
ATC:	"Cessna three four Bravo squawk 4223 and Ident."
You:	You do as directed.
ATC:	"Cessna three four Bravo radar contact, maintain VFR, I'll get back to you."
You:	"Three four Bravo."
Later...	
ATC:	"Cessna three four Bravo descend and maintain 3,000, fly heading 010, vector straight-in VOR approach runway 19 at Concord, information Charlie is current.
You:	"Three four Bravo, we have Charlie, leaving 3,500 for 3,000, heading 010."

As soon at ATC tells you to <u>maintain</u> 3,000 feet you are now on an IFR flight plan. The remainder is simple, fly the headings and altitudes assigned, shoot the approach and land.

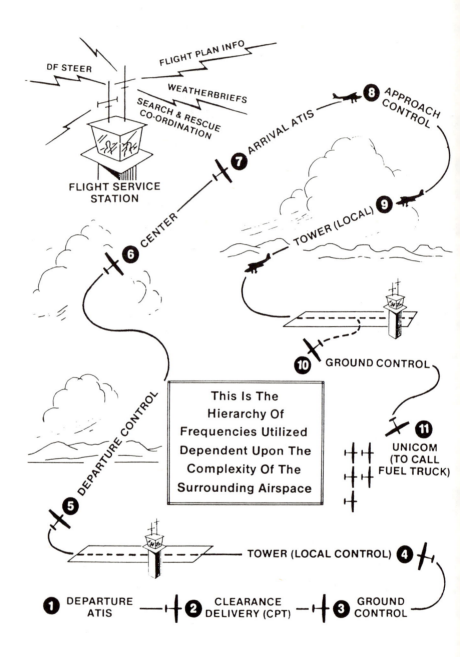

DF STEER

FLIGHT PLAN INFO

WEATHERBRIEFS

SEARCH & RESCUE
CO-ORDINATION

FLIGHT SERVICE
STATION

8 APPROACH CONTROL

7 ARRIVAL ATIS

9 TOWER (LOCAL)

6 CENTER

10 GROUND CONTROL

DEPARTURE CONTROL

This Is The
Hierarchy Of
Frequencies Utilized
Dependent Upon The
Complexity Of The
Surrounding Airspace

11 UNICOM
(TO CALL
FUEL TRUCK)

5 DEPARTURE CONTROL

TOWER (LOCAL CONTROL) **4**

1 DEPARTURE ATIS — **2** CLEARANCE DELIVERY (CPT) — **3** GROUND CONTROL

Page 210

GLOSSARY

These pages comprise a Pilot/Controller glossary of commonly used terms. In addition to many of the definitions found in the Airman's Information Manual glossary are some terms that have yet to be included. Refer to the AIM for an expanded and updated version as new terms are constantly being added.

ABEAM — An aircraft is "abeam" a fix, point or object when that fix, point or object is approximately 90 degrees to the right or left of the aircraft track. Abeam indicates a general position rather than a precise point.

ABORT — To terminate a preplanned aircraft maneuver; e.g., an aborted takeoff.

ACKNOWLEDGE — Let me know that you have received and understand my message.

ADVISE INTENTIONS — Tell me what you plan to do.

ADVISE GROUND OF FIRST VECTOR FIX — At large, busy airports Ground Control does not have the time to look at the clearance that each aircraft was issued. The ATIS will include instructions to "Advise Ground of first vector fix" so that Ground Control can assign the most expeditious runway to departing traffic. Your first vector fix is usually the closest VOR in your departure instructions.

ADVISORY — Advise and information provided to assist pilots in the safe conduct of flight and aircraft movement (See Advisory Service)

ADVISORY FREQUENCY — The appropriate frequency to be used for Airport Advisory Service.

ADVISORY SERVICE — Advise and information provided by a facility to assist pilots in the safe conduct of flight and aircraft movement.

AERIAL REFUELING/IN-FLIGHT REFUELING — A procedure used by the military to transfer fuel from one aircraft to another during flight.

AERODROME — A defined area on land or water (including any buildings, installations and equipment) intended to be used either wholly or in part for the arrival, departure, and movement of aircraft.

An AERODROME is another name for the airport.

AFFIRMATIVE — Yes.

(Affirm is a shortened form and has the same meaning.)

AIRCRAFT — Device/s that are used or intended to be used for flight in the air and when used in air traffic control terminology may include the flight crew.

AIRCRAFT APPROACH CATEGORY — A grouping of aircraft based on a speed of 1.3 times the stall speed in the landing configuration at maximum gross landing weight. An aircraft shall fit in only one category. If it is necessary to maneuver at speeds in excess of the upper limit of a speed range for a category, the minimums for the next higher category should be used. For example, an aircraft which falls in Category A, but is circling to land at a speed in excess of 91 knots, should use the approach Category B minimums when circling to land. The categories are as follows:

1. Category A — Speed less than 91 knots.

2. Category B — Speed 91 knots or more but less than 121 knots.

3. Category C — Speed 121 knots or more but less than 141 knots.

4. Category D — Speed 141 knots or more but less than 166 knots.

5. Category E. — Speed 166 knots or more.

(Refer to FAR Parts 1 and 97)

AIRCRAFT CLASSES — For the purposes of Wake Turbulence Separation Minima, ATC classifies aircraft as Heavy, Large and Small as follows:

1. Heavy — Aircraft capable of takeoff weights of 300,000 pounds or more whether or not they are operating at this weight during a particular phase of flight.

2. Large — Aircraft of more than 12,500 pounds, maximum certificated takeoff weight, up to 300,000 pounds.

3. Small — Aircraft of 12,500 pounds or less, maximum certificated takeoff weight.

AIRMET/AIRMAN'S METEOROLOGICAL INFORMATION — Inflight weather advisories which cover moderate icing, moderate turbulence, sustained winds of 30 knots or more within 2,000 feet of the surface and the initial onset of phenomena producing extensive areas of visibilities below 3 miles or ceilings less than 1,000 feet. It concerns weather phenomena which are of operational interest to all aircraft and potentially hazardous to aircraft having limited capability because of lack of equipment, instrumentation or pilot qualifications. It concerns weather of less severity than SIGMETs or convective SIGMETs.

AIRPORT — An area of land or water that is used or intended to be used for the landing and takeoff or aircraft and includes its buildings and facilities, if any.

AIRPORT ADVISORY AREA — the area within ten miles of an airport without a control tower or where the tower is not in operation and on which a flight service station is located.

AIRPORT ADVISORY SERVICE/AAS — A service provided by Flight Service Stations at airports not served by a control tower. This service consists of providing information to arriving and departing aircraft concerning wind direction and speed, favored runway, altimeter setting, pertinent known traffic, pertinent known field conditions, airport taxi routes and traffic patterns, and authorized instrument approach procedures. This information is advisory in nature and does not constitute an ATC clearance.

AIRPORT ELEVATION/FIELD ELEVATION — The highest point of an airport's usable runways measured in feet from mean sea level.

AIRPORT ROTATING BEACON — A visual NAVAID operated at many airports. At civil airports, alternating white and green flashes indicate the location of the airport. At military airports, the beacons flash alternately white and green, but are differentiated from civil beacons by dualpeaked (two quick) white flashes between the green flashes.

AIRPORT SURFACE DETECTION EQUIPMENT/ ASDE — Radar equipment specifically designed to detect all principal features on the surface of an airport including aircraft and vehicular traffic and to present the entire image on a radar indicator console in the control tower. Used to augment visual observation by tower personnel of aircraft and/or vehicular movements on runways and taxiways.

AIRPORT TRAFFIC AREA — Unless otherwise specifically designated in FAR Part 93, that airspace within a horizontal radius of 5 statute miles from the geographical center of any airport at which a control tower is operating, extending from the surface up to, but not including, an altitude of 3,000 feet above the elevation of the airport. Unless otherwise authorized or required by ATC, no person may operate an aircraft within an airport traffic area except for the purpose of landing at, or taking off from, an airport within the area. ATC authorizations may be given as individual approval of specific operations or may be contained in written agreements between airport users and the tower concerned.

AIRSPEED — The speed of an aircraft relative to its surrounding air mass. the unqualified term "airspeed" means one of the following:

1. Indicated Airspeed — The speed shown on the aircraft airspeed indicator. This is the speed used in pilot/ controller communications under the general term "airspeed."

2. True Airspeed — The airspeed of an aircraft relative to undisturbed air. Used primarily in flight planning and en route portion of flight. When used in pilot/controller communications, it is referred to as "true airspeed" and not shortened to "airspeed."

AIRSTART — The starting of an aircraft engine while the aircraft is airborne, preceded by engine shutdown during training flights or by actual engine failure.

AIR TRAFFIC — Aircraft operating in the air or on an airport surface, exclusive of loading ramps and parking areas.

ALERT NOTICE/ALNOT — A message sent by a flight Service Station (FSS) or Air Route Traffic Control Center (ARTCC) that requests an extensive communication search for overdue, unreported, or missing aircraft.

ALPHA-NUMERIC DISPLAY/DATA BLOCK — Letters and numerals used to show identification, altitude, beacon code, and other information concerning a target on a radar display.

ALTERNATE AIRPORT — An airport at which an aircraft may land if a landing at the intended airport becomes inadvisable.

ALTIMETER SETTING — The barometric pressure reading used to adjust a pressure altimeter for variations in existing atmospheric pressure or to the standard altimeter setting (29.92).

ALTITUDE — The height of a level, point, or object measured in feet Above Ground Level AGL) or from Mean Sea Level (MSL).

1. MSL Altitude — Altitude expressed in feet measured from mean sea level.

2. AGL Altitude — Altitude expressed in feet measured above ground level.

3. Indicated Altitude — the altitude as shown by an altimeter. On a pressure or barometric altimeter it is altitude as shown uncorrected for instrument error and uncompensated for variation from standard atmosheric conditions.

ALTITUDE READOUT/AUTOMATIC ALTITUDE REPORT — An aircraft's altitude, transmitted via the Mode C transponder feature, that is visually displayed in 100-foot increments on a radar scope having readout capability.

ALTITUDE RESTRICTION — An altitude or altitudes stated in the order flown which are to be maintained until reaching a specific point or time. Altitude restrictions may be issued by ATC due to traffic, terrain, or other airspace considerations.

ALTITUDE RESTRICTIONS ARE CANCELED — Adherence to previously imposed altitude restrictions is no longer required during a climb or descent.

APPROACH CLEARANCE — Authorization by ATC for a pilot to conduct an instrument approach. The type of instrument approach for which clearance and other pertinent information is provided in the approach clearance when required.

APPROACH GATE — The point on the final approach course which is 1 mile from the final approach fix on the side away from the airport or 5 miles from landing threshold, whichever is farther from the landing threshold. This is an imaginary point used within ATC as a basis for final approach course interception for aircraft being vectored to the final approach course. Also called Arrival Gate.

Approach Speed — The recommended speed contained in aircraft manuals used by pilots when making an approach to landing. This speed will vary for different segments of an approach as well as for aircraft weight and configuration.

APRON/RAMP — A defined area, on a land airport, intended to accomodate aircraft for purposes of loading or unloading passengers or cargo, refueling, parking or maintenance. With regard to seaplanes, a ramp is used for access to the apron from the water.

ARC — The track over the ground of an aircraft flying at a constant distance from a navigational aid by reference to distance measuring equipment (DME).

AREA NAVIGATION/RNAV — A method of navigation that permits aircraft operations on any desired course within the coverage of station-referenced navigation signals or within the limits of self-contained system capability.

ARRESTING SYSTEM — A safety device consisting of two major components, namely, engaging or catching devices, and energy absorption devices for the purpose of arresting both tail hook and/or non-tail hook equipped aircraft. It is used to prevent aircraft from overrunning runways when the aircraft cannot be stopped after landing or during aborted takeoff. Arresting systems have various names, e.g., arresting gear, hook, device, wire, barrier cable.

ARRIVAL TIME — The time an aircraft touches down on arrival.

ATC ADVISES — Used to prefix a message of noncontrol information when it is relayed to an aircraft by other than an air traffic controller.

ATC CLEARS — Used to prefix an ATC clearance when it is relayed to an aircraft by other than an air traffic controller.

ATC INSTRUCTION — Directives issued by air traffic control for the purpose of requiring a pilot to take specific actions; e.g., "Turn left heading two five zero", "Go around," "Clear the runway."

ATC REQUESTS — Used to prefix an ATC request when it is relayed to an aircraft by other than an air traffic controller.

AUTOMATED RADAR TERMINAL SYSTEMS/ARTS — The generic term of the ultimate in functional capability afforded by several automation systems. Each differs in functional capabilities and equipment. ARTS plus a suffix roman Numeral denotes a specific system. A following letter indicates a major modification to that system. In general, an ARTS displays for the terminal controller aircraft identification, flight plan data, other flight associated information, e.g., altitude and speed, and aircraft position symbols in conjunction with his radar presentation. Normal radar co-exists with the alphanumeric display. In addition to enhancing visualization of the air traffic situation, ARTS facilitate intra/inter-facility transfer and coordination of flight information. These capabilities are enabled by specially designed computers and subsystems tailored to the radar and communications equipments and operational requirements of each automated facility. Modular design permits adoption of improvements in computer software and electronic technologies as they become available while retaining the characteristics unique to each system.

See the Airman's Information Manual for an expanded description of the ARTS system.

AUTOMATIC TERMINAL INFORMATION SERVICE/ATIS — The continuous broadcast of recorded noncontrol information in selected terminal areas. Its purpose is to improve controller effectiveness and to relieve frequency congestion by automating the repetitive transmission of essential but routine information, e.g., "Los Angeles information Alpha. One three zero zero Greenwich, Weather, measured ceiling two thousand overcast, visibility three, haze, smoke, temperature seven one, wind two five zero at five, altimeter two niner niner six. I-L-S Runway Two Five Left Approach in use, Runway Two Five Right closed, advise you have Alpha."

BACK TAXI — To return to the runway threshold by using the active runway as a taxiway. Back taxi instructions are usually accompanied by instructions to "hold in position" or by take-off clearance.

BELOW MINIMUMS — Weather conditions below the minimums prescribed by regulation for the particular action involved, e.g., landing minimums, takeoff minimums.

BLAST FENCE — A barrier that is used to divert or dissipate jet or propeller blast.

BLIND SPOT/BLIND ZONE — An area from which radio transmissions and/or radar echoes cannot be received. The term is also used to describe portions of the airport not visibile from the control tower.

BLOCK ALTITUDE — The assignment by ATC of a Block Altitude refers to an altitude assignment that is variable. The aircraft may maneuver between the floor and ceiling designated in the block. For example a block altitude may be assigned between 15,000 and 19,000 and it would be permissable for the aircraft to fly anywhere in between those altitudes. Block altitudes are usually requested by jet pilots for training purposes and also for aircraft desiring altitude flexibility to avoid weather.

BRAKING ACTION (GOOD, FAIR, POOR, OR NIL) — A report of conditions on the airport movement area providing a pilot with a degree/quality of braking that he might expect. Braking action is reported in terms of good, fair, poor or nil.

BREAK OFF YOUR APPROACH — Discontinue your IFR approach and fly away from the final approach course. These instructions are followed by instructions to enter the normal traffic pattern VFR.

BROADCAST — Transmission of information for which an acknowledgement is not expected.

CALL-UP — Initial voice contact between a facility and an aircraft, using the identification of the unit being called and the unit initiating the call.

CARDINAL ALTITUDES OR FLIGHT LEVELS — "Odd" or "Even" thousand-foot altitudes or flight levels; e.g., 5,000, 6,000, 7,000, FL 250, FL 260, FL 270.

CEILING — The height above the earth's surface of the lowest layer of clouds or obscuring phenomena that is reported as "broken," "overcast," or "obscuration," and not classified as "thin" or "partial".

CENTER STORED — A term used extensively in Canada. It means the same as "As filed". Example — "Three four Bravo cleared via Center stored."

CIRCLE TO LAND MANEUVER/CIRCLING MANEUVER — A maneuver initiated by the pilot to align the aircraft with a runway for landing when a straight-in landing from an instrument approach is not possible or is not desirable. This maneuver is made only after ATC authorization has been obtained and the pilot has established required visual reference to the airport.

CIRCLE TO RUNWAY (RUNWAY NUMBERED) — Used by ATC to inform the pilot that he must circle to land becuase the runway in use is other than the runway aligned with the instrument approach procedure. When the direction of the circling maneuver in relation to the airport/runways is required, the controller will state the direction (eight cardinal compass points) and specify a left or right downwind or base leg as appropriate, e.g., "Cleared VOR Runway three six approach circle to Runway two two" or "Circle northwest of the airport for a right downwind to Runway two two."

CLEAR-AIR TURBULANCE/CAT — Turbulence encountered in air where no clouds are present. This term is commonly applied to high-level turbulence associated with wind shear. CAT is often encounted in the vicinity of the jet stream.

CLEARANCE LIMIT — The fix, point, or location to which an aircraft is cleared when issued an air traffic clearance.

CLEARANCE VOID IF NOT OFF BY (TIME) — Used by ATC to advise an aircraft that the departure clearance is automatically canceled if takeoff is not made prior to a specified time. The pilot must obtain a new clearance or cancel his IFR flight plan if not off by the specified time.

COMPANY TRAFFIC — A term used by ATC to advise converging traffic that they both work for the same company.

COMPASS ROSE — A circle, graduated in degrees, printed on some charts or marked on the ground at an airport. It is used as a reference to either true or magnetic direction.

COMPULSORY REPORTING POINTS — Reporting points which must be reported to ATC. They are designated on aeronautical charts by solid triangles or filed in a flight plan as fixes selected to define direct routes. These points are geographical locations which are defined by navigation aides/fixes. Pilots should discontinue position reporting over compulsory reporting points when informed by ATC that their aircraft is in "radar contact."

CONTACT —
1. Establish communications with (followed by the name of the facility and, if appropriate, the frequency to be used).

2. A flight condition wherein the pilot ascertains the attitude of his aircraft and navigates by visual reference to the surface.

CONTACT APPROACH — An approach wherein an aircraft on an IFR flight plan, having an air traffic control authorization, operating clear of clouds with at least 1 mile flight visibility and a reasonable expectation of continuing to the destination airport in those conditions, may deviate from the instrument approach procedure and proceed to the destination airport by visual reference to the surface. This approach will only be authorized when requested by the pilot and the *reported ground visibility* at the destination is at least 1 statute mile.

CONTROLLED AIRSPACE — Airspace designated as a continental control area, control area, control zone, terminal control area, transition area, or positive control area within which some or all aircraft may be subject to air traffic control.

CLEARED AS FILED — Means the aircraft is cleared to proceed in accordance with the route of flight filed in the flight plan. This clearance does not include the altitude, SID, or SID Transition.

CLEARED FOR (Type Of) APPROACH — ATC authorization for an aircraft to execute a specific instrument approach procedure to an airport; e.g., "Cleared for ILS Runway Three Six Approach."

CLEARED FOR APPROACH — ATC authorization for an aircraft to execute any standard or special instrument approach procedure for that airport. Normally, an aircraft will be cleared for a specific instrument approach procedure

CLEARED FOR TAKEOFF — ATC authorization for an aircraft to depart. It is predicated on known traffic and known physical airport conditions.

CLEARED FOR THE OPTION — ATC authorization for an aircraft to make a touch-and-go, low approach, missed approach, stop and go, or full stop landing at the discretion of the pilot. It is normally used in training so that an instructor can evaluate a student's performance under changing situations.

CLEARED THROUGH — ATC authorization for an aircraft to make intermediate stops at specified airports without refiling a flight plan while en route to the clearance limit.

CLEARED TO LAND — ATC authorization for an aircraft to land. It is predicated on known traffic and known physical airport conditions.

CLEARWAY — An area beyond the takeoff runway under the control of airport authorities within which terrain or fixed obstacles may not extend above specified limits. These areas may be required for certain turbine powered operators and the size and upward slope of the clearway will differ depending on when the aircraft was certificated.

CLIMBOUT — That portion of flight operation between takeoff and the initial cruising altitude.

CLIMB TO VFR — ATC authorization for an aircraft to climb to VFR conditions within a control zone when the only weather limitation is restricted visibility. The aircraft must remain clear of clouds while climbing to VFR.

CLOSED RUNWAY — A runway that is unusable for aircraft operations. Only the airport management/military operations office can close a runway.

CLOSED TRAFFIC — Successive operations involving takeoffs and landings or low approaches where the aircraft does not exit the traffic pattern.

CLUTTER — In radar operations clutter refers to the reception and visual display of radar returns caused by precipitation, chaff, terrain, numerous aircraft targets,or other phenomena. Such returns may limit or preclude ATC providing services based on radar.

CODES/TRANSPONDER CODES — The number assigned to a particular multiple pulse reply signal transmitted by the transponder.

CONTROL SECTOR — An airspace area of defined horizontal and vertical dimensions for which a controller, or group of controllers, has air traffic control responsibility, normally within an air route traffic control center or an appraoch control facility. Sectors are established based on predominant traffic flows, altitude strata, and controller workload. Pilot-communications during operations within a sector are normally maintained on discrete frequencies assigned to the sector.

CONTROL SLASH — A radar beacon slash representing the actual position of the associated aircraft. Normally, the control slash is the one closest to the interrogating radar beacon site. When ARTCC radar is operating in narrowband (digitized) mode, the control slash is converted to a target symbol.

CONVECTIVE SIGMET/**CONVECTIVE SIGNIFICANT METEOROLIGICAL INFORMATION** — A weather-advisory concerning convective weather significant to the safety of all aircraft. Convective SIGMETs are issued for tornadoes, lines of thunderstorms, embedded thunderstorms of any intensity level, isolated thunderstoms for intensity level 5 and above, areas of thunderstorms containing intensity level 4 and above, and hail ¾ inch or greater.

COORDINATES — The intersection of lines of reference, ususally expressed in degrees/minutes/seconds of latitude and longitude, used to determine position or location.

COORDINATION FIX — The fix in relation to which facilities will handoff, transfer control of an aircraft, or coordinate flight progress date. For terminal facilities, it may also serve as a clearance for arriving aircraft.

CORRECTION — An error has been made in the transmission and the correct version follows:

COURSE —

1. The intended direction of flight in the horizontal plane measured in degrees from north.

2. The ILS localizer signal pattern usually specified as front course or back course.

CROSS (FIX) AT (ALTITUDE) — Used by ATC when a specific altitude restriction at a specified fix is required.

CROSS (FIX) AT OR ABOVE (ALTITUDE) — Used by ATC when an altitude restriction at a specified fix is required. It does not prohibit the aircraft from crossing the fix at a higher altitude than specified; however, the higher altitude may not be one that will violate a succeeding altitude restriction or altitude assignment.

CROSS (FIX) AT OR BELOW (ALTITUDE) — Used by ATC when a maximum crossing altitude at a specific fix is required. It does not prohibit the aircraft from crossing the fix at a lower altitude; however, it must be at or above the minimum IFR altitude.

CROSSING TRAFFIC — Traffic is crossing in front of you. This phrase is usually accompanied by the direction, "left to right" or "right to left".

CROSSWIND —

1. When used concerning the traffic pattern, the word means "crosswind leg."

2. When used concerning wind conditions, the word means a wind not parallel to the runway or the path of an aircraft.

CROSSWIND COMPONENT — The wind component measured in knots at 90 degrees to the longitudinal axis of the runway.

CRUISE — Used in an ATC clearance to authorize a pilot to conduct flight at any altitude from the minimum IFR altitude up to and including the altitude specified in the clearance. The pilot may level off at any intermediate altitude within this block of airspace. Climb/descend within the block is to be made at the discretion of the pilot. However, once the pilot starts descent and verbally reports leaving an altitude in the block he may not return to that altitude without additional ATC clearance. Further, it is approval for the pilot to proceed to and make an approach at destination airport and can be used in conjunction with:

1. An airport clearance limit at locations with a standard/special instrument approach procedure. The FARs require that if an instrument letdown to an airport is necessary the pilot shall make the letdown in accordance with a standard/special instrument approach procedure for that airport, or

2. An airport clearance limit at locations that are within/ below/outside controlled airspace and without a standard/special instrument approach procedure. Such a clearance is NOT AUTHORIZATION for the pilot to descent under IFR conditions below the applicable minimum IFR altitude nor does it imply that ATC is exercising control over aircraft in uncontrolled airspace; however, it provides a means for the aircraft to proceed to destination airport, descent, and land in accordance with applicable FARs governing VFR flight operations. Also, this provides search and rescue protection until such time as the IFR flight plan is closed.

CRUISING ALTITUDE/LEVEL — An altitude or flight level maintained during en route level flight. This is a constant altitude and should not be confused with a cruise clearance.

DECISION HEIGHT/DH — With respect to the operation of aircraft, means the height at which a decision must be made during an ILS or PAR instrument approach to either continue the approach or to execute a missed approach.

DELAY INDEFINITE (REASON IF KNOWN) EXPECT FURTHER CLEARANCE (TIME) — Used by ATC to inform a pilot when an accurate estimate of the delay time and the reason for the delay cannot immediately be determined; e.g., a disabled aircraft on the runway, terminal or center area saturation, weather below landing minimums, etc.

DELAY VECTOR — A heading assignment that "stalls for time", usually for approach sequencing.

DEPARTURE CONTROL — A function of an approach control facility providing air traffic control service for departing IFR and, under certain conditions, VFR aircraft.

DEPARTURE TIME — The time an aircraft becomes airborne.

DEVIATIONS —

1. A departure from a current clearance, such as an off course maneuver to avoid weather or turbulence.

2. Where specifically authorized in the FAR's and requested by the pilot, ATC may permit pilots to deviate from certain regulations.

DF APPROACH PROCEDURE — Used under emergency conditions where another instrument approach procedure cannot be executed. DF guidance for an instrument approach is given by ATC facilities with DF capability.

DF FIX — The geographical location of an aircraft obtained by one or more direction finders..

DF GUIDANCE/DF STEER — Headings provided to aircraft by facilities equipped with direction finding equipment. These headings, if followed, will lead the aircraft to a predetermined point such as the DF station or an airport. DF guidance is given to aircraft in distress or to other aircraft which request the service. Practice DF guidance is provided when workload permits.

DIRECT — Straight line flight between two navigational aids, fixes, points, or any combination thereof. When used by pilots in describing off-airway routes, points defining direct route segments become compulsory reporting points unless the aircraft is under radar contact.

DISABLED AIRCRAFT — An aircraft that is unable to move on it's own. Such as an aircraft with a blown tire.

DISCRETE CODE/DISCRETE BEACON CODE — As used in the Air Traffic Control Radar Beacon System (ATCRBS), any one of the 4096 selectable Mode 3/A aircraft transponder codes except those ending in zero zero; e.g., discrete codes: 0010, 1201, 2317, 7777; non-discrete codes: 0100, 1200, 7700. Non-discrete codes are normally reserved for radar facilities that are not equipped with discrete decoding capability and for other purposes such as emergencies (7700), VFR aircraft (1200), etc.

DISCRETE FREQUENCY — A separate radio frequency for use in direct pilot-controller communications in air traffic control which reduces frequency congestion by controlling the number of aircraft operating on a particular frequency at one time. Discrete frequencies are normally designated for each control sector in en route/terminal ATC facilities. Discrete frequencies are listed in the Airport/Facility Directory, and DOD FLIP IFR En Route Supplement.

DISPLACED THRESHOLD — A threshold that is located at a point on the runway other than the designated beginning of the runway.

DISTANCE MEASURING EQUIPMENT/DME — Equipment (airborne and ground) used to measure, in nautical miles, the slant range distance of an aircraft from the DME navigational aid.

DISTRESS — A condition of being threatened by serious and/or imminent danger, and of requiring immediate assistance.

EN ROUTE FLIGHT ADVISORY SERVICE/FLIGHT WATCH — A service specifically designed to provide, upon pilot request, timely weather information pertinent to his type of flight, intended route of flight, and altitude. The FSSs providing this service are listed in Airport/Facility Directory.

EXECUTE MISSED APPROACH — Instructions issued to a pilot making an instrument approach which means continue inbound to the missed approach point and execute the missed approach procedure as described on the Instrument Approach Procedure Chart, or as previously assigned by ATC. The pilot may climb immediately to the altitude specified in the missed approach procedure upon making a missed approach. No turns should be initiated prior to reaching the missed approach point. When conducting an ASR or PAR approach, execute the assigned missed approach procedure immediately upon receiving instructions to "execute missed approach."

EXPECT (ALTITUDE) AT (TIME) of (FIX) — Used under certain conditions in a departure clearance to provide a pilot with an altitude to be used in the event of two-way communication failure.

EXPECT DEPARTURE CLEARANCE (TIME)/EDCT — Used in Fuel Advisory Departure (FAD) program. The time the operator can expect a gate release. Excluding long distance flights, and EDCT will always be assigned even though it may be the same as the Estimated Time of Departure (ETD). The EDCT is calculated by adding the ground delay factor.

EXPECT FURTHER CLEARANCE (TIME) /EFC — The time a pilot can expect to receive clearance beyond a clearance limit.

EXPECT FURTHER CLEARANCE VIA (AIRWAYS, ROUTES OR FIXES) — Used to inform pilot of the routing he can expect if any part of the route beyond a short range clearance limit differs from that filed.

EXPEDITE — Used by ATC when prompt compliance is required to avoid the development of an imminent situation.

FERRY FLIGHT — A flight for the purpose of:

1. Returning an aircraft to base.

2. Delivering an aircraft from one location to another.

3. Moving an aircraft to and from a maintenance base.

Ferry flights, under certain conditions may be conducted under terms of a special flight permit.

FILED — Normally used in conjunction with flight plans meaning a flight plan has been submitted to ATC.

FINAL — Commonly used to mean that an aircraft is on the final approach course or is aligned with a landing area.

FINAL APPROACH COURSE — A straight line extension of a localizer, a final approach radial/bearing, or a runway centerline, all without regard to distance.

FINAL APPROACH FIX/FAF — The designated fix from or over which the final approach (IFR) to an airport is executed. The FAF identifies the beginning of the final approach segment of the instrument approach.

FINAL APPROACH-IFR — The flight path of an aircraft which is inbound to an airport on a final instrument approach course, beginning at the final approach fix or point and extending to the airport or the point where a circle to land maneuver or a missed approach is executed.

FINAL CONTROLLER — The controller providing information and final approach guidance during PAR and ASR approaches utilizing radar equipment.

FIX — A geographical position determined by visual reference to the surface, by reference to one or more radio NAVAIDs, by celestial plotting, or by another navigational device.

FLIGHT INSPECTION/FLIGHT CHECK — Inflight investigation and evaluation of a navigational aid to determine whether it meets established tolerances.

FLIGHT LEVEL — A level of constant atmospheric pressure related to a reference datum of 29.92 inches of mercury. Each is stated in three digits that represent hundreds of feet. For example, flight level 250 represents a barometric altimeter indication of 25,000 feet; flight level 255, an indication of 25,500 feet.

FLIGHTS OF TWO (FLIGHT LEADER) — Formation flight of two aircraft. (A flight of three would be three aircraft.) Usually one aircraft is the flight leader and he communicates with ATC for himself and the entire group. Common in the military.

FLIGHT PATH — A line, course, or track along which an aircraft is flying or intended to be flown.

FLIGHT PLAN — Specified information relating to the intended flight of an aircraft that is filed orally or in writing with a FSS or an ATC facility.

FLIGHT PLAN ROUTE — The route you filed on your written flight plan. If altered instructions had been issued during one portion of your flight and ATC desired you to continue the remainder of your flight as filed, the term "flight plan route" is often substituted.

FLIGHT SERVICE STATION/FSS — Air traffic facilities which provide pilot briefing, en route communications and VFR search and rescue services, assist lost aircraft and aircraft in emergency situations, relay ATC clearances, originate Notices to Airmen, broadcast aviation weather and NAS information, receive and process IFR flight plans, and monitor NAVAIDS. In addition, at selected locations FSSs provide Enroute Flight Advisory Service (Flight Watch), take weather observations, issue airport advisories, and advise Customs and Immigration of transborder flights.

FLIGHT TEST — A flight for the purpose of:

1. Investigating the operation/flight characteristics of an aircraft or aircraft component.

2. Evaluating an applicant for a pilot certificate or rating.

FLIGHT WATCH — A shortened term for use in airground contacts on frequency 122.0 MHz to identify the flight service station providing En Route Flight Advisory Service; e.g., "Oakland Flight Watch." 134.825 High Altitude.

FLOW CONTROL — Measures designed to adjust the flow of traffic into a given airspace, along a given route, or bound for a given aerodrome (airport) so as to ensure the most effective utilization of the airspace.

FLY HEADING (DEGREES) — Informs the pilot of the heading he should fly. The pilot may have to turn to, or continue on, a specific compass direction in order to comply with the instructions. The pilot is expected to turn in the shorter direction to the heading, unless otherwise instructed by ATC.

FORMATION FLIGHT — More than one aircraft which, by prior arrangement between the pilots, operate as a single aircraft with regard to navigation and position reporting. Separation between aircraft within the formation is the responsibility of the flight leader and the pilots of the other aircraft in the flight. This includes transition periods when aircraft within the formation are maneuvering to attain separation from each other to effect individual control and during join-up and breakaway.

1. A standard formation is one in which a proximity of no more than 1 mile laterally or longitudinally and within 100 feet vertically from the flight leader is maintained by each wingman.

2. Nonstandard formations are those operating under any of the following conditions:

   a. When the flight leader has requested and ATC has approved other than standard formation dimensions.

   b. When operating within an authorized altitude reservation (ALTRV) or under the provisions of a Letter of Agreement.

   c. When the operations are conducted in airspace specifically designed for a special activity.

FUEL ADVISORY DEPARTURE/FAD — Procedures to minimize engine running time for aircraft destined for an airport experiencing prolonged arrival delays.

FUEL DUMPING — Airborne release of usable fuel. This does not include the dropping of fuel tanks.

FUEL SIPHONING/FUEL VENTING — Unintentional release of fuel caused by overflow, puncture, loose cap, etc.

GATE HOLD PROCEDURES — Procedures at selected airports to hold aircraft at the gate or other ground location whenever departure delays exceed or are anticipated to exceed 5 minutes. The sequence for departure will be maintained in accordance with initial call up unless modified by Flow Control restrictions. Pilots should monitor the ground control/clearance delivery frequency for engine startup advisories or new proposed start time if the delay changes.

GLIDE PATH (ON/ABOVE/BELOW) — Used by ATC to inform an aircraft making a PAR approach of its vertical position (elevation) relative to the descent profile. The terms "slightly" and "well" are used to describe the degrees of deviation, e.g., "slightly above glidepath." Trend information is also issued with respect to the elevation of the aircraft and may be modified by the terms "rapidly" and "slowly," e.g., "well above glidepath, coming down rapidly."

GO AHEAD — Proceed with your message. Not to be used for any other purpose.

GO AROUND — Instructions for a pilot to abandon his approach to landing. Additional instructions may follow. Unless otherwise advised by ATC, a VFR aircraft or an aircraft conducting a visual approach should overfly the runway while climbing to traffic pattern altitude and enter the traffic pattern via the crosswind leg. A pilot on an IFR flight plan making an instrument approach should execute the published missed approach procedure or proceed as instructed by ATC, e.g., "Go around" (additional instructions, if required).

GOOD TIME — A modern phrase that means the same as "without delay", or "hurry up." Example — "Three four Bravo cross the right, then contact Ground, good time please."

GROUND CLUTTER — A pattern produced on the radar scope by ground returns which may degrade other radar returns in the affected area. The effect of ground clutter is minimized by the use of moving target indicator (MTI) circuits in the radar equipment resulting in a radar presentation which displays only targets which are in motion.

GROUND CONTROLLED APPROACH/GCA — A radar approach system operated from the ground by air traffic control personnel transmitting instructions to the pilot by radio. The approach may be conducted with surveillance radar (ASR) only or with both surveillance and precision approach radar (PAR). Usage of the term "GCA" by pilots is discouraged except when referring to a GCA facility. Pilots should specifically request a "PAR" approach when a precision radar approach is desired, or request an "ASR" or "surveillance" approach when a nonprecision radar approach is desired.

GUARD FREQUENCY — The same as VHF 121.5 or UHF 243.0 the MAYDAY frequency. A clear channel that ATC facilities monitor for aircraft in distress. Example — "Aircraft transmitting on Guard say again your call sign."

HANDOFF — An action taken to transfer the radar identification of an aircraft from one controller to another if the aircraft will enter the receiving controller's airspace and radio communications with the aircraft will be transferred.

HAVE NUMBERS — Used by pilots to inform ATC that they have received runway, wind, and altimeter information only.

HIGH SPEED TAXIWAY/EXIT/TURNOFF — A long radius taxiway designed and provided with lighting or marking to define the path of aircraft, traveling at high speed (up to 60 knots), from the runway center to a point on the center of a taxiway. Also referred to as long radius exit or turn-off taxiway. The high speed taxiway is designed to expedite aircraft turning off the runway after landing, thus reducing runway occupancy time.

HOLD/HOLDING PROCEDURE — A predetermined maneuver which keeps aircraft within a specified airspace while awaiting further clearance from air traffic control. Also used during ground operations to keep aircraft within a specified area or at a specified point while awaiting further clearance from air traffic control.

HOLDING FIX — A specified fix identifiable to a pilot by NAVAIDS or visual reference to the ground used as a reference point in establishing and maintaining the position of an aircraft while holding.

HOMING — flight toward a NAVAID, without correcting for wind, by adjusting the aircraft heading to maintain a relative bearing of zero degrees.

HOT — The joint-use airspace is unusable for civil aircraft at this time. Example — "R-2525 is Hot today."

HOW DO YOU HEAR ME? — A question relating to the quality of the transmission or to determine how well the transmission is being received.

IDENT — A request for a pilot to activate the aircraft transponder identification feature. This will help the controller to confirm an aircraft identity or to identify an aircraft.

IDENT FEATURE — The special feature in the Air traffic Control Radar Beacon System (ATCRBS) equipment. It is used to immediately distinguish one displayed beacon target from other beacon targets.

IF NO TRANSMISSION RECEIVED FOR (TIME) — Used by ATC in radar approaches to prefix procedures which should be followed by the pilot in event of lost communications.

IFR AIRCRAFT/IFR FLIGHT — An aircraft conducting flight in accordance with instrument flight rules.

IFR CONDITIONS — Weather conditions below the minimum for flight under visual flight rules.

IMMEDIATELY — Used by ATC when such action compliance is required to avoid an imminent situation.

INSTRUMENT FLIGHT RULES/IFR — Rules governing the procedures for conducting instrument flight. Also a term used by pilots and controllers to indicate type of flight plan.

INSTRUMENT METEOROLOGICAL CONDITIONS — IMC — Meteorological conditions expressed in terms of visibility, distance from cloud, and ceiling less than the minima specified for visual meteorological conditions.

INSTRUMENT RUNWAY — A runway equipped with electronic and visual navigation aids for which a precision or nonprecision approach procedure having straight-in landing minimums has been approved.

INTERSECTING RUNWAYS — Two or more runways which cross or meet within their lengths.

INTERSECTION —

1. A point defined by any combination of courses, radials, or bearings of two or more navigational aids.

2. Used to describe the point where two runways cross, a taxiway and a runway cross, or two taxiways cross.

INTERSECTION DEPARTURE/INTERSECTION TAKEOFF — A takeoff or proposed takeoff on a runway from an intersection.

I SAY AGAIN — The message will be repeated.

JAMMING — Electronic or mechanical interference which may disrupt the display of aircraft on radar or the transmission/reception of radio communications/navigation.

JET BLAST — Jet engine exhaust (thrust stream turbulence).

JET ROUTE — A route designed to serve aircraft operations from 18,000 feet MSL up to and including flight level 450. The routes are referred to as "J" routes with numbering to identify the designated route, e.g., J 105.

KNOWN TRAFFIC — With respect to ATC clearances, means aircraft whose altitude, position, and intentions are known to ATC.

LANDING ROLL — The distance from the point of touchdown to the point where the aircraft can be brought to a stop or exit the runway.

LANDING SEQUENCE — The order in which aircraft are positioned for landing.

LIGHT GUN — A handheld directional light signaling device which emits a brilliant narrow beam of white, green or red light as selected by the tower controller. The color and type of light transmitted can by used to approve or disapprove anticipated pilot actions where radio communication is not available. The light gun is used for controlling traffic operating in the vicinity of the airport and on the airport movement area.

LOCAL TRAFFIC — Aircraft operating in the traffic pattern or within sight of the tower, or aircraft known to be departing or arriving from flight in local practice areas, or aircraft executing practice instrument approaches at the airport.

LOST COMMUNICATIONS/TWO-WAY RADIO COMMUNICATIONS FAILURE — Loss of the ability to communicate by radio. Aircraft are sometimes referred to as NORDO (No Radio). Standard pilot procedures are specified in FAR Part 91. Radar controllers issue procedures for pilots to follow in the event of lost communications during a radar approach when weather reports indicate that an aircraft will likely encounter IFR weather conditions during the approach.

LOW APPROACH — An approach over an airport or runway following an instrument approach or a VFR approach including the go-around maneuver where the pilot intentionally does not make contact with the runway.

MAINTAIN —

1. Concerning altitude/flight level, the term means to remain at the altitude/flight level specified. The phrase "climb and" or "descend and" normally precedes "maintain" and the altitude assignment, e.g. "descend and maintain 5,000.

2. Concerning other ATC instructions, the term is used in its literal sense, e.g., maintain VFR.

3. Restating previously issued altitude to "MAINTAIN" is an ammended clearance. If altitude to "MAINTAIN" is changed or restated, whether prior to departure or while airborne, and the previously issued altitude restrictions are ommitted, ALTITUDE RESTRICTIONS ARE CANCELED, including SID altitude restrictions, if any.

MAKE SHORT APPROACH — Used by ATC to inform a pilot to alter his traffic pattern so as to make a short final approach.

MAYDAY — The international radiotelephony distress signal. When repeated three times, it indicates imminent and grave danger and that immediate assistance is requested.

METERING — A method of time regulating arrival traffic flow into a terminal area so as not to exceed a predetermined terminal acceptance rate.

MINIMUM FUEL — Indicates that an aircraft's fuel supply has reached a state where, upon reaching the destination, it can accept little or no delay. This is not an emergency situation but merely indicates an emergency situation is possible should any undue delay occur.

MISSED APPROACH —

1. A maneuver conducted by a pilot when an instrument approach cannot be completed to a landing. The route of flight and altitude are shown on instrument approach procedure charts. A pilot executing a missed approach prior to the Missed Approach Point (MAP) must continue along the final approach to the MAP. The pilot may climb immediately to the altitude specified in the missed approach procedure.

2. A term used by the pilot to inform ATC that he is executing the missed approach.

3. At locations where ATC radar service is provided, the pilot should conform to radar vectors, when provided by ATC, in lieu of the published missed approach procedure.

MISSED APPROACH POINT/MAP — A point described in each instrument approach procedure at which a missed approach procedure shall be executed if the required visual reference does not exist.

MODE — The letter or number assigned to a specific pulse spacing of radio signals transmitted or received by ground interrogator or airborne transponder components of the Air Traffic Control Radar Beacon System (ATCRBS). Mode A (military Mode 3) and Mode C (altitude reporting) are used in air traffic control.

NEGATIVE — "No," or "permission not granted," or "that is not correct."

NEGATIVE CONTACT —
Used by pilots to inform ATC that:

1. Previously issued trafic is not in sight. It may be followed by the pilot's request for the controller to provide assistance in avoiding the traffic.

2. They were unable to contact ATC on a particular frequency

NIGHT — The time between the end of evening civil twilight and the beginning of morning civil twilight, as published in the American Air Almanac, converted to local time.

NO GYRO APPROACH/VECTOR — A radar approach/ vector provided in case of a malfunctioning gyrocompass or directional gyro. Instead of providing the pilot with headings to be flown, the controller observes the radar track and issues control instructions "turn right/left" or "stop turn," as appropriate.

NONAPPROACH CONTROL TOWER — Authorizes aircraft to land or takeoff at the airport controlled by the tower, or to transit the airport traffic area. The primary function of a nonapproach control tower is the sequencing of aircraft in the traffic pattern and on the landing area. Nonapproach control towers also separate aircraft operating under instrument flight rules clearances from approach controls and centers. They provide ground control services to aircraft, vehicles, personnel, and equipment on the airport movement area.

NORDO — No radio contact has been established. Example — "Aircraft on downwind is Nordo."

NUMEROUS TARGETS VICINITY (LOCATION) — A traffic advisory issued by ATC to advise pilots that targets on the radar scope are too numerous to issue individually.

NUMBER ONE FOR TAKE-OFF — You are the next in line for take-off. You are the aircraft closest to the double yellow hold line.

OFFSET PARALLEL RUNWAYS — Staggered runways having centerlines which are parallel.

ON COURSE —

1. Used to indicate that an aircraft is established on the route centerline.

2. Used by ATC to advise a pilot making a radar approach that his aircraft is lined up on the final approach course.

ON-COURSE INDICATION — An indication on an instrument which provides the pilot a visual means of determining that the aircraft is located on the centerline of a given navigational track, or an indication on a radar scope that an aircraft is on a given track.

OPTION APPROACH — An approach requested and conducted by a pilot which will result in either a touch-and-go, missed approach, low approach, stop-and-go, or full stop landing.

OUT — The conversation is ended and no response is expected.

OVER — My transmission is ended; I expect a response.

OVERHEAD APPROACH/360 OVERHEAD — A series of predetermined maneuvers prescribed for VFR arrival of military aircraft (often in formation) for entry into the VFR traffic pattern and to proceed to a landing. The pattern usually specifies the following.

1. The radio contact required of the pilot.

2. The speed to be maintained.

3. An initial approach 3 to 5 miles in length.

4. An elliptical pattern consisting of two 180 degree turns.

5. A break point at which the first 180 degrees turn is started.

6. The direction of turns.

7. Altitude (at least 500 feet above the conventional pattern).

8. A "Roll-out" on final approach not less than ¼ mile from the landing threshold and not less than 300 feet above the ground.

PAN — The international radio-telephony urgency signal. When repeated three times indicates uncertainty or alert, followed by nature of urgency.

PAINTING CELL — A cell is the core of a thunderstorm. When ATC observes a cell on his scope his advisory often uses the term "painting" to describe radar's recognition of the cell.

PARALLEL ILS APPROACHES — ILS approaches to parallel runways by IFR aircraft which, when established inbound toward the airport on the adjacent localizer courses, are radar-separated by at least 2 miles.

PARALLEL OFFSET ROUTE — A parallel track to the left or right of the designated or established airway/route. Normally associated with Area Navigation (RNAV) operations.

PARALLEL RUNWAYS — Two or more runways at the same airport whose centerlines are parallel. In addition to runway number, parallel runways are designated as L (left) and R (right) or, if three parallel runways exist, L (left), C (center), and R (right).

PILOT'S DISCRETION — When used in conjunction with altitude assignments, means that ATC has offered the pilot the option of starting climb or descent whenever he wishes and conducting the climb or descent at any rate he wishes. He may temporarily level off at any intermediate altitude. However, once he has vacated an altitude he may not return to that altitude.

PILOT WEATHER REPORT/PIREP — A report of meteorological phenomena encountered by aircraft in flight.

POSITION REPORT/PROGRESS REPORT — A report over a known location as transmitted by an aircraft to ATC.

POSITIVE CONTROL — The separation of all air traffic, within designated airspace, by air traffic control.

PRACTICE INSTRUMENT APPROACH — An instrument approach procedure conducted by a VFR or IFR aircraft for the purpose of pilot training or proficiency demonstrations.

PRECIPITATION — Any or all forms of water particles (rain, sleet, hail, or snow) that fall from the atmosphere and reach the surface.

PRECISION APPROACH PROCEDURE/PRECISION APPROACH — A standard instrument approach procedure in which an electronic glide slope is provided, e.g., ILS and PAR.

PROCEDURE TURN INBOUND — That point of a procedure turn maneuver where course reversal has been completed and an aircraft is established inbound on the intermediate approach segment or final approach course. A report of "procedure turn inbound" is normally used by ATC as a position report for separation purposes.

PROFILE DESCENT — An uninterrupted descent (except where level flight is required for speed adjustment, e.g., 250 knots at 10,000 feet MSL) from cruising altitude/level to interception of a glide slope or to a minimum altitude specified for the initial or intermediate approach segment of a non-precision instrument approach. The profile descent normally terminates at the approach gate or where the glide scope or other appropriate minimum altitude is intercepted.

QUICK LOOK — A feature of NAS Stage A and ARTS which provides the controller the capability to display full data blocks of tracked aircraft from other control positions.

RADAR ARRIVAL — An arriving aircraft which is being vectored to the final approach course for an instrument approach or for a visual approach to the airport.

RADAR CONTACT —

1. Used by ATC to inform an aircraft that it is identified on the radar display and radar flight following will be provided until radar identification is terminated. Radar service may also be provide within the limits of necessity and capability. When a pilot is informed of "radar contact," he automatically discontinues reporting over compulsory reporting points.

2. A term used to inform the controller initiating a handoff that the aircraft is identified and approval is granted for the aircraft to enter the receiving controller's airspace.

RADAR CONTACT LOST — Used by ATC to inform a pilot that radar identification of his aircraft has been lost. The loss may be attributed to several things including the aircraft merging with weather or ground clutter, the aircraft flying below radar line of sight, the aircraft entering an area of poor radar return, or a failure of the aircraft transponder or ground radar equipment.

RADAR ENVIRONMENT — An area in which radar service may be provided.

RADAR FLIGHT FOLLOWING — The observation of the progress of radar identified aircraft, whose primary navigation is being provided by the pilot, wherein the controller retains and correlates the aircraft identity with the appropriate target or target symbol displayed on the radar scope.

RADAR IDENTIFICATION — The process of ascertaining that an observed radar target is the radar return from a particular aircraft.

RADAR SERVICE TERMINATED — Used by ATC to inform a pilot that he will no longer be provided any of the services that could be received while under radar contact. Radar service is automatically terminated and the pilot is not advised in the following cases:

1. An aircraft, cancels its IFR flight plan, except within a TCA, TRSA, or where Stage II service is provided.

2. At the completion of a radar approach.

3. When an arriving VFR aircraft, receiving radar services, is advised to contact the tower.

4. When an aircraft conducting a visual approach or contact approach is advised to contact the tower.

5. When an aircraft making an instrument approach has landed or the tower has the aircraft in sight, whichever occurs first.

RADIAL — A magnetic bearing extending from a VOR/VORTAC/TACAN navigation facility.

RADIO —

1. A device used for communication.

2. Used to refer to a Flight Service Station, e.g., "Seattle Radio" is used to call Seattle FSS.

ROGER — I hear you, I heard you. Technically, I have received all of your last transmission. It should not be used to answer a question requiring a yes or a no.

ROLLING — A term used by jet pilots to acknowlege take-off clearance because jets are somewhat slow to initially accelerate.

ROUTE — A defined path, consisting of one or more courses in a horizontal plane, which aircraft traverse over the surface of the earth.

RUNWAY PROFILE DESCENT — An instrument flight rules (IFR) air traffic control arrival procedure to a runway published for pilot use in graphic and/or textual form and may be associated with a STAR. Runway Profile Descents provide routing, and may depict crossing altitudes, speed restrictions, and headings to be flown from the en route structure to the point where the pilot will receive clearance for and execute an instrument approach procedure. A Runway Profile Descent may apply to more than one runway if so stated on the chart.

SAY AGAIN — Used to request a repeat of the last transmission. Usually specifies transmission or portion thereof not understood or received, e.g., "Say again all after ABRAM VOR."

SAY ALTITUDE — Used by ATC to ascertain an aircraft's special altitude/flight level. When the aircraft is climbing or descending, the pilot should state the indicated altitude rounded to the nearest 100 feet.

SAY HEADING — Used by ATC to request an aircraft's heading. The pilot should state the actual heading of the aircraft.

SEE AND AVOID — A visual procedure wherein pilots of aircraft flying in visual meteorological conditions (VMC), regardless of type of flight plan, are charged with the responsibility to observe the presence of other aircraft and to maneuver their aircraft as required to avoid the other aircraft. Right-of-way rules are contained in FAR, Part 91. (See Instrument Flight Rules, Visual Flight Rules, Visual Meteorological Conditions, Instrument Meteorological Conditions)

SEGMENTED CIRCLE — A system of visual indicators designed to provide traffic pattern information at airports without operating control towers.

SEPARATION — In air traffic control, the spacing of aircraft to achieve their safe and orderly movement in flight and while landing and taking off.

SHORT PATTERN — To turn crosswind and downwind sooner than expected by the tower. Example — "Request short pattern."

SIDESTEP MANEUVER — A visual maneuver accomplished by a pilot at the completion of an instrument approach to permit a straight-in landing on a prarallel runway not more than 1200 feet to either side of the runway to which the instrument approach was conducted.

SIMULTANEOUS ILS APPROACHES — An approach system permitting simultaneous ILS approaches to airports having parallel runways separated by at least 4,300 feet between centerlines. Integral parts of a total system are ILS, radar, communications, ATC procedures, and appropriate airborne equipment.

SLOW TAXI — To taxi a float plane at low power or low RPM.

SPEAK SLOWER — Used in verbal communications as a request to reduce speech rate.

SPECIAL EMERGENCY — A condition of air piracy, or other hostile act by a person(s) aboard an aircraft, which threatens the safety of the aircraft or its passengers.

SPECIAL VFR CONDITIONS — Weather conditions in a control zone which are less than basic VFR and in which some aircraft are permitted flight under Visual Flight Rules.

SPECIAL VFR OPERATIONS — Aircraft operating in accordance with clearances within control zones in weather conditions less than the basic VFR weather minima. Such operations must be requested by the pilot and approved by ATC.

SPEED ADJUSTMENT — An ATC procedure used to request pilots to adjust aircraft speed to a specific value for the purpose of providing desired spacing. Speed adjustments are expected to maintain a speed of plus or minus 10 knots of the specified speed.

Examples of Speed Adjustments are:

1. "Increase speed to (speed)," or "Increase speed (number of) knots" — Used by ATC to request a pilot to increase the indicated airspeed of the aircraft.

2. "Reduce speed to (speed)" or "Reduce speed (number of) knots" — Used by ATC to request a pilot to reduce the indicated airspeed of the aircraft.

3. "If feasible, reduce speed to (speed)," or "If feasible, reduce speed (number of) knots" — Used by ATC to request a pilot to reduce the indicated airspeed of the aircraft below specified speeds.

SQUAWK (Mode, Code, Function) — Activate specific modes/codes/functions on the aircraft transponder, e.g., "Squawk three/alpha, two one zero five, low."

STANDARD INSTRUMENT DEPARTURE/SID —A preplanned instrument flight rule (IFR) air traffic control departure procedure printed for pilot use in graphic and/or textual form. SIDs provide transition from the terminal to the appropriate en route structure.

STANDARD RATE TURN — A turn of three degrees per second.

STANDARD TERMINAL ARRIVAL/STAR — A preplanned instrument flight rule (IFR) air traffic control arrival procedure published for pilot use in graphic and/or textual form. STARs provide transition from the en route structure to an outer fix or an instrument approach fix/arrival waypoint in the terminal area.

STAND BY — Means the controller or pilot must pause for a few seconds, usually to attend to other duties of a higher priority. Also means to wait as in "standy by for clearance." If a delay is lengthy, the caller should reestablish contact.

STAY WITH ME — Do not change frequencies.

STOP ALTITUDE SQUAWK — Used by ATC to inform an aircraft to turn-off the automatic altitude reporting feature of its transponder. It is issued when the verbally reported altitude varies 300 feet or more from the automatic altitude report.

STOP AND GO — A procedure wherein an aircraft will land, make a complete stop on the runway, and then commence a takeoff from that point.

STOP SQUAWK (Mode or Code) — Used by ATC to tell the pilot to turn specified functions of the aircraft transponder off.

STOPWAY — An area beyond the takeoff runway designated by the airport authorities as able to support an airplane during an aborted takeoff.

STRAIGHT-IN APPROACH — IFR — An instrument approach wherein final approach is begun without first having executed a procedure turn; not necessarily completed with a straight-in landing or made to straight-in landing minimums.

STRAIGHT-IN APPROACH — VFR — Entry into the traffic pattern by interception of the extended runway centerline (final approach course) without executing any other portion of the traffic pattern.

STRAIGHT-IN LANDING — A landing made on a runway aligned within 30 degrees of the final approach course following completion of an instrument approach.

SUNSET AND SUNRISE — The mean solar times of sunset and sunrise as published in the Nautical Almanac, converted to local standard time for the locality concerned. Within Alaska, the end of evening civil twilight and the beginning of morning civil twilight, as defined for each locality.

SURVEILLANCE APPROACH — An instrument approach wherein the air traffic controller issues instructions for pilot compliance based on aircraft position in relation to the final approach course (azimuth) and the distance (range) from the end of the runway as displayed on the controller's radar scope. The controller will provide recommended altitudes on final approach if requested by the pilot.

TARGET — The indication shown on a radar display resulting from a primary radar return or a radar beacon reply.

TAXI BACK — A phrase used by ATC after an aircraft has executed a full stop landing and wishes to taxi back to the active runway for another take-off. ATC usually issues taxi back instructions with the added phrase, "remain this frequency." (meaning do not switch to Ground, stay with me...)

TAXI INTO POSITION AND HOLD — Used by ATC to inform a pilot to taxi onto the departure runway in takeoff position and hold. It is not authorization for takeoff. It is used when takeoff clearance cannot immediately be issued because of traffic or other reasons.

TAXIWAY DEPARTURE — Using the taxiway as a runway to depart an airport. When approved by ATC, the taxiway is given a number as if it were an official runway. Example — "Taxiway 18 departure approved, cleared for take-off."

TERMINAL AREA — A general term used to describe airspace in which approach control service or airport traffic control service is provided.

TERMINAL RADAR PROGRAM — A national program instituted to extend the terminal radar services, provided IFR aircraft, to VFR aircraft. Pilot participation in the program is urged but not mandatory. The program is divided into two parts and referred to as Stage II and Stage III. The Stage service provided at a particular location is contained in Airport/Facility Directory.

1. Stage I originally comprised two basic radar services (traffic advisories and limited vectoring to VFR aircraft). These services are provided by all commissioned terminal radar facilities, but the term "Stage I" has been deleted from use.

2. Stage II/Radar Advisory and Sequencing for VFR Aircraft — Provides, in addition to traffic advisories, vectoring and sequencing on a full-time basis to arriving VFR aircraft.The purpose is to adjust the flow of arriving IFR and VFR aircraft into the traffic pattern in a safe and orderly manner and to provide traffic advisory to departing VFR aircraft.

3. Stage III/Radar Sequencing and Separation Service for VFR Aircraft — Provides, in addition to traffic advisories and Stage II services, separation between all participating aircraft. The purpose is to provide separation between all participating VFR aircraft and all IFR aircraft operating within the airspace defined as a Terminal Radar Service Area (TRSA) or Terminal Control Area (TCA).

TERMINAL RADAR SERVICE AREA/TRSA — Airspace surrounding designated airports wherein ATC provides radar vectoring, sequencing, and separation on a fulltime basis for all IFR and participating VFR aircraft. Service provided in TRSA is called Stage III Service. AIM contains an explanation of TRSA. Graphics depicting TRSA layout and communications frequencies are shown in Graphic Notices and Supplemental Data. Pilot participation is urged but is not mandatory.

TETRAHEDRON — A device normally located on uncontrolled airports and used as a landing direction indicator. The small end of a tetrahedron points in the direction of landing. At controlled airports, the tetrahedron, if installed, should be disregarded because tower instructions supersede the indicator.

THAT IS CORRECT — The understanding you have is right.

THRESHOLD — The beginning of that portion of the runway usable for landing.

TOUCH AND GO/TOUCH AND GO LANDING — An operation by an aircraft that lands and departs on a runway without stopping or exiting the runway.

TOUCHDOWN —

1. The point at which an aircraft first makes contact with the landing surface.

2. Concerning a precision radar approach (PAR), it is the point where the glide path intercepts the landing surface.

TOWER/AIRPORT TRAFFIC CONTROL TOWER
— A terminal facility that uses air/ground radio communications, visual signaling, and other devices to provide ATC services to aircraft operating in the vicinity of an airport or on the movement area. Authorizes aircraft to land.

TOWER EN ROUTE CONTROL SERVICE/TOWER TO TOWER — The control of IFR en route traffic within delegated airspace between two or more adjacent approach control facilities. This service is designed to expedite traffic and reduce control and pilot communication requirements.

TRACK — The actual flight path of an aircraft over the surface of the earth.

TRAFFIC —

1. A term used by a controller to transfer radar identification of an aircraft to another controller for the purpose of coordinating separation action. Traffic is normally used (a) in response to a handoff or point out, (b) in anticipation of a handoff or point out, or (c) in conjunction with a request for control of an aircraft.

2. A term used by ATC to refer to one or more aircraft.

TRAFFIC ADVISORIES — Advisories issued to alert a pilot to other known or observed air traffic which may be in such proximity to his aircraft's position or intended route of flight to warrent his attention. Such advisories may be based on:

1. Visual observation from a control tower.

2. Observation of radar identified and nonidentified aircraft targets on an ATC radar display, or

3. Verbal reports from pilots or other facilities.

Controllers use the word "traffic" followed by additional information, if known, to provide such advisories, e.g., "Traffic, 2 o'clock one zero miles, southbound, fast moving, eight thousand." Traffic advisory service will be provided to the extent possible depending on higher priority duties of the controller or other limitations, e.g., radar limitations, volume of traffic, frequency congestion, or controller workload. Radar/nonradar traffic advisories do not relieve the pilot of his responsibility to see and avoid other aircraft. Pilots are cautioned that there are many times when the controller is not able to give traffic advisories concerning all traffic in the aircraft's proximity; in other words, when a pilot requests or is receiving traffic advisories, he should not assume that all traffic will be issued.

TRAFFIC FAST MOVING — A relative judgement call by ATC. Usually is meant to convey that the traffic is moving much faster than you. The traffic will be converging at a rapid rate.

TRAFFIC IN SIGHT — Used by pilots to inform a controller that previously issued traffic is in sight.

TRAFFIC NO LONGER A FACTOR — Indicates that the traffic described in a previously issued traffic advisory is no longer a factor.

TRAFFIC PATTERN — The traffic flow that is prescribed for aircraft landing at, taxiing on, or taking off from an airport. The components of a typical traffic pattern are upwind leg, crosswind leg, downwind leg, base leg, and final approach.

1. Upwind Leg — A flight path parallel to the landing runway in the direction of landing.

2. Crosswind Leg — A flight path at right angles to the landing runway off its upwind end.

3. Downwind Leg — A flight path parallel to the landing runway in the direction opposite to landing. The downwind leg normally extends between the crosswind leg and the base leg.

4. Base Leg — A flight path at right angles to the landing runway off its approach end. the base leg normally extends from the downwind leg to the intersection of the extended runway centerline.

5. Final Approach — A flight path in the direction of landing along the extended runway centerline. The final approach normally extends from the base leg to the runway. An aircraft making a straight-in approach VFR is also considered to be on final approach.

TRANSCRIBED WEATHER BROADCAST/TWEB — A continuous recording of meteorological and aeronautical information that is broadcast on L/MF and VOR facilities for pilots.

TRANSMISSOMETER — An apparatus used to determine visibility by measuring the transmission of light through the atmosphere. It is the measurement source for determining runway visual range (RVR) and runway visibility value (RVV).

TRANSMITTING IN THE BLIND/BLIND TRANSMISSION — A transmission from one station to other stations in circumstances where two-way communication cannot be established, but where it is believed that the called stations may be able to receive the transmission.

TRANSPONDER — The airborne radar beacon receiver/transmitter portion of the Air Traffic Control Radar Beacon System (ATCRBS) which automatically receives radio signals from interrogators on the ground, and selectively replies with a specific reply pulse or pulse group only to those interrogations being received on the mode to which it is set to respond.

TURBOJET AIRCRAFT — An aircraft having a jet engine in which the energy of the jet operates a turbine which in turn operates the air compressor.

TURBOPROP AIRCRAFT — An aircraft having a jet engine in which the energy of the jet operates a turbine which drives the propeller.

UNABLE — Indicates inability to comply with a specific instruction, request, or clearance.

UNCONTROLLED AIRSPACE — Uncontrolled airspace is that portion of the airspace that has not been designated as continental control area, control areas, control zone, terminal control area, or transition area and within which ATC has neither the authority nor the responsibility for exercising control over air traffic.

UNICOM — A non-government communication facility which may provide airport information at certain airports. Locations and frequencies of UNICOMs are shown on aeronautical charts and publications.

UNPUBLISHED ROUTE — A route for which no minimum altitude is published or charted for pilot use. It may include a direct route between NAVAIDS, a radial, a radar vector, or a final approach course beyond the segments of an instrument approach procedure.

URGENCY — A condition of being concerned about safety, and of requiring timely but not immediate assistance; a potential Distress condition.

VECTOR — A heading issued to an aircraft to provide navigational guidance by radar.

VERIFY — Request confirmation of information, e.g., "verify assigned altitude."

VERIFY SPECIFIC DIRECTION OF TAKEOFF (OR TURNS AFTER TAKEOFF) — Used by ATC to ascertain an aircraft's direction of takeoff and/or direction of turn after takeoff. It is normally used for IFR departures from an airport not having a control tower. When direct communications with the pilot is not possible, the request and information may be relayed through an FSS, dispatcher, or by other means.

VFR AIRCRAFT/VFR FLIGHT — An aircraft conducting flight in accordance with visual flight rules.

VFR CONDITIONS — Weather conditions equal to or better than the minimum for flight under visual flight rules. The term may be used as an ATC clearance/instruction only when:

1. An IFR aircraft requests a climb/descent in VFR conditions.

2. The clearance will result in noise abatement benefits where part of the IFR departure route does not conform to an FAA approved noise abatement route or altitude.

3. A pilot has requested a practice instrument approach and is not on an IFR flight plan.

All pilots receiving this authorization must comply with the VFR visibility and distance from cloud criteria in FAR Part 91. Use of the term does not relieve controllers of their responsibility to separate aircraft in TCAs/TRSAs as required by FAA Handbook 7110.65. When used as an ATC clearance/instruction, the term may be abbreviated "VFR;" e.g., "Maintain VFR," "Climb/descend VFR," etc.

VFR CONDITIONS ON-TOP/VFR-ON-TOP — ATC authorization from an IFR aircraft to operate in VFR conditions at any appropriate VFR altitude (as specified in FAR and as restricted by ATC). A pilot receiving this authorization must comply with the VFR cloud criteria, and the minimum IFR altitudes specified in *VFR ON TOP/VFR CONDITIONS ON TOP* — An IFR clearance term used in lieu of a specific altitude assignment upon pilot's request which authorizes the aircraft to be flown in VFR weather conditions at an appropriate VFR altitude which is not below the minimum IFR altitude.

VFR OVER THE TOP — The operation of an aircraft above the clouds under VFR when it is not being operated on an IFR flight plan.

VISIBILITY — The ability, as determined by atmospheric conditions and expressed in units of distance, to see and identify prominent unlighted objects by day and prominent lighted objects by night. Visibility is reported as statute miles, hundreds of feet, or meters.

1. Flight Visibility — The average forward horizontal distance, from the cockpit of an aircraft in flight, at which prominent unlighted objects may be seen and identified by day and prominent lighted objects may be seen and identified at night.

2. Ground Visibility — Prevailing horizontal visibility near the earth's surface as reported by the United States National Weather Service or an accredited observer.

3. Prevailing Visibility — The greatest horizontal visibility equaled or exceeded throughout at least half the horizon circle which need not necessarily be continuous.

4. Runway Visibility Value/RVV — The visibility determined for a particular runway by a transmissometer. A meter provides a continuous indication of the visibility (reported in miles or fraction of miles) for the runway. RVV is used in lieu of prevailing visibility in determining minimums for a particular runway.

5. Runway Visual Range/RVR — An instrumentally derived value, based on standard calibrations, that represent the horizontal distance a pilot will see down the runway from the approach end. It is based on the sighting of either high intensity runway lights or on the visual contrast of other targets, whichever yields the greater visual range. RVR, in contrast to prevailing or runway visibility, is based on what a pilot in a moving aircraft should see looking down the runway. RVR is horizontal visual range, not slant visual range. It is based on the measurement of a transmissometer made near the touchdown point of the instrument runway and is reported in hundreds of feet. RVR is used in lieu of RVV and/or prevailing visibility in determining minimums for a particular runway.

a. Touchdown RVR — The RVR visibility readout values obtained from RVR equipment serving the runway touchdown zone.

b. Mid-RVR — The RVR readout values obtained from RVR equipment located midfield of the runway.

c. Rollout RVR — The RVR readout values obtained from RVR equipment located nearest the rollout end of the runway.

VISUAL APPROACH — An approach wherein an aircraft on an IFR flight plan, operating in VFR conditions under the control of an air traffic control facility and having an air traffic control authorization, may proceed to the airport of destination in VFR conditions.

VISUAL FLIGHT RULES/VFR — Rules that govern the procedures for conducting flight under visual conditions. The term "VFR" is also used in the United States to indicate weather conditions that are equal to or greater than minimum VFR requirements. In addition, it is used by pilots and controllers to indicate type of flight plan.

VISUAL HOLDING — The holding of aircraft at selected, prominent, geographical fixes which can be easily recognized from the air.

VISUAL METEOROLOGICAL CONDITIONS/ VMC — Meteorological conditions expressed in terms of visibility, distance from cloud, and ceiling equal to or better than specified minima.

VISUAL SEPARATION — A means employed by ATC to separate aircraft in terminal areas. There are two ways to effect this separation:

1. The tower controller sees the aircraft involved and issues instructions, as necessary, to ensure that the aircraft avoid each other.

2. A pilot sees the other aircraft involved and upon instruction from the controller provides his own separation by maneuvering his aircraft, as necessary, to avoid it. This may involve following another aircraft or keeping it in sight until it is no longer a factor.

VOT/VOR TEST SIGNAL — A ground facility which emits a test signal to check VOR receiver accuracy. The system is limited to ground use only.

WAKE TURBULENCE — Phenomena resulting from the passage of an aircraft through the atmosphere. The term includes vortices, thrust steam turbulence, jet blast, jet wash, propeller wash, and rotor wash both on the ground and in the air.

WEATHER ADVISORY/WS/WQ — In aviation weather forecast practice, an expression of hazardous weather conditions not predicted in the area forecast as they affect the operation of air traffic and as prepared by the NWS.

WILCO — I have received your message, understand it, and will comply with it.

WIND SHEAR — A change in wind speed and/or wind direction in a short distance resulting in a tearing or shearing effect. It can exist in a horizontal or vertical direction and occasionally in both.

WORDS TWICE —

1. As a request, "Communication is difficult. Please say every phase twice."

2. As information, "Since communications are difficult, every phrase in this message will be spoken twice."